GOD PLAYS A PURPLE BANJO

Mary
Peace & Joy!

Sam

GOD PLAYS A PURPLE BANJO

and 41 Other Stories
of Inspiration,
Hope and Humor

S. JAMES MEYER

TWENTY-THIRD
PUBLICATIONS
twentythirdpublications.com

IN GRATITUDE FOR MY PARENTS,

RON AND JUDY MEYER,

THE OAKEN STOCK FROM

WHICH I WAS HEWN.

TWENTY-THIRD PUBLICATIONS
One Montauk Avenue, Suite 200
New London, CT 06320
(860) 437-3012 or (800) 321-0411
www.twentythirdpublications.com

Cover photo: © iStockphoto.com / RapidEye

ISBN: 978-1-62785-442-9
Library of Congress Control Number: 2018962303
Printed in the U.S.A.

 A division of Bayard, Inc.

CONTENTS

PART 4: EXAMINATION

PART 5: JUBILATION

PART 6: CONTEMPLATION

BEFORE THE BEGINNING

Three hundred fifty-three high school students sat on folding chairs in the gym. Some yawned. A few got a little rowdy. No one wanted to be there except for the handful who were really into religion. An all-school Mass had just concluded, but everyone was asked to remain while the principal walked to the microphone and introduced a guest speaker.

The students all knew who he was. Percy Walsch owned and operated Spirit Haus, a liquor store on the east side. He was a big supporter of the school and sent birthday cards to each of the seniors when they turned eighteen, along with a coupon to save ten percent on "graduation supplies." It was 1981, and the legal drinking age was eighteen, so no one bothered to give this practice a second thought. Actually, a couple of years later, the state legislature did give it a second thought and moved the legal drinking age to twenty-one. Percy still sent cards and coupons to all the seniors, but the new coupons noted that Spirit Haus also sold ice and soda.

Percy lowered the microphone about eleven inches and cleared his throat: "Before I begin speaking, I'd like to say something." That's all I remember from that day. I recall nothing about the Mass or about Percy Walsch's message to the students. I only remember his grammatical snafu, which informed us that once he began speaking, he would have nothing to say.

This was the church of my youth—honest and sincere, yet often confused and searching for something to say. It meant well, but we could never be sure if it was serving the people or itself. We sat in chairs because we were told to, registering little beyond the ironies and contradictions. As a result, I believe many of us became observers rather than participants. We didn't reject faith, we just didn't connect with the church. We were searching for meaning and direction in this life while our pastors and religion teachers were telling us to worry about the next life.

Somehow along the way, wise people introduced me to a deeper concept of faith, a church that, like the incarnation of Jesus himself, unifies the ideas of heaven and earth. I wrote this book in that spirit. The division between sacred and secular, I wholeheartedly believe, is false and dangerous. Each breath, each moment, each person is a sacred revelation of God among us. Hopefully, these stories will illuminate just how extraordinary your ordinary days are, how very sacred each breath, each moment, and each person is.

Authors often advise readers on how to read a book such as this. They'll suggest you read one story a day and then meditate on its application in your life, sometimes giving you self-guided reflection questions. I'm not going to do that. Skip around, start in the back, draw numbers randomly, devour it like a bucket of popcorn, or sip it like hot tea. It's organized by seasons, so some stories may seem more relevant at certain times than others, but life isn't as tidy as a church calendar. We often experience moments of incarnation on Monday, the deserts of Lent on Wednesday, and the joy of resurrection on Friday, all in the same week.

Part One

PREPARATION

Red-Headed Dumplings

ODELIA MEYER MADE THE WORLD'S BEST RED-HEADED DUMP-LINGS. At least that's what everyone claimed. I can't say for sure because I've never tasted anyone else's red-headed dumplings. Nor would I want to. For those unfamiliar with rural German culinary arts, red-headed dumplings are pretty much deep-fried bread/egg balls smothered in gravy. There is so much simultaneously right and wrong with the whole idea. Anytime you deep fry anything and pour gravy over it, you've entered the conceptual tension between good and evil. If Jesus and Lucifer ever had dinner together, I imagine there would be red-headed dumplings on the table. And probably Lambrusco. It's the sort of thing that levels the playing field because everyone is equally confused about whether or not it's OK.

Growing up, they were *the* staple of every extended Meyer family event. After Grandma passed away, the women in the family politically maneuvered to identify who would prepare the dumplings. Actually, I don't know that for sure. I might be making it up. But I want to believe that making the red-headed dumplings for a large extended family gathering was both a privilege and a curse. This is a family of over seventy good-natured, wise-cracking, opinionated people. If they disapproved of something, they would tell you everything wrong with it. If they approved of something, they would still tell you everything wrong with it, but they'd smile more.

Everyone in the family agreed that the red-headed dumplings were delicious, but I don't honestly know if they were agreeing in fact or idea. In fact, they were good, but they weren't oh-my-God-the-world-can-stop-spinning good. They certainly weren't worth the level of praise ladled upon them by people who ordinarily save praise for draft horses. It's the memory of Grandma and a deep reverence for how much she valued large family meals that made them delicious. Red-headed dumplings place Grandma directly in our midst. You can feel her. It is as though she is within you and all around you. Her story is our story.

Eucharist is like this. It's not going to mean a whole lot if we don't know Christ. I don't mean know of him or know about him. I mean really know Christ. Red-headed dumplings have meaning because of who Grandma was and what values she passed to us. Eucharist has meaning because of who Christ is. If it wasn't for everything he said and did, everything he brought to the very first Eucharist, there would be nothing sacred about any of this. It all would have been forgotten long ago.

So what did Jesus bring? Well, he brought everything and laid it all on the table. He said, listen, we're not going to experience God's kingdom unless we pour our hearts into it. Here, I'll go first. Now it's your turn. You do the same.

I think he's still waiting for us to go.

The Catholic Liturgy of the Eucharist begins with the Offertory for a reason. This is the bold statement of what we're willing to lay on the table to experience God's kingdom. What's it worth to us? Jesus showed us what he was willing to ante up. His body and his blood. And then he went out and did it.

The preparation question we face is, how much of our own blood, sweat, and tears are we putting into the cup? Eucharist has very little meaning if we're holding any part of ourselves back. Bring it all, Jesus says. Pour your heart out...your hopes, your dreams, your struggles, your pains, your joy, your deep-fried emptiness, and then smother it all in the gravy of love. Lay it all on the table so that the Holy Spirit can come upon it and turn it all into the body of Christ.

ഗ്രൂഡ്ഡ് ഗ്രൂഡ്ഡ് · ഡ്ഡ്ഡ്ഡ്ഡ്ഡ്ഡ്

Dueling Car Seats

I WAS QUITE SURE I HAD LIFE FIGURED OUT. After all, at twenty-five, I had my first good job, a cute wife on my arm, and I was living the lyrics of John Mellencamp—*driving around with the car top down and the radio on.* If self-satisfied smugness is a sin, I was its dark prince. Michelle and I would notice people our age with children, and we'd snicker at their double-barrel strollers and dueling car seats. No thank you. We were living large.

And then one Sunday afternoon, we were at our favorite ice cream shop and I noticed Michelle was looking past me with a strange gaze in her eyes. I peered over my shoulder and saw an infant giggling in its mother's arms. I turned back. Michelle's iron-melting eyes were now fixed on me. By the time my head stopped spinning, I was at the car dealership trading in my freedom for a cherry-red minivan with built-in juice-box holders.

I was changing. Not just on the outside, but on the inside. My sense of self, my identity, was changing. I would walk out in public proudly swinging a Pooh Bear diaper bag and flip a spit rag over my shoulder like I had once carried soccer cleats. My perspectives and priorities were changing. This one little life was having a profound impact on me. Michelle, of course, was going through a similar identity shift, but it seemed so natural with her. She had always been a gentle, nurturing soul; I had not.

Sometimes I wonder if parenthood changed Mary and Joseph. How could it not? Did they feel as ill-equipped and inadequate as I did? I imagine they felt as joyful and thankful, but did they also feel as unworthy and insecure? And then I wonder...what if they weren't the first people God asked? Simply asking the question feels a little sacrilegious, but what if Mary wasn't the first person God asked to bring Christ into the world? What if God had been asking people all along, but Mary was the first with the faith, courage, and heart to say yes? And what if Mary wasn't the last? What if God has been asking each of us ever since, "Will you change your vision for yourself and give me life within you?"

In the gospel, people are all abuzz. They share our eagerness as they await their savior. "What should we do? How should we prepare?" they ask John the Baptist. And John says, "Flood Facebook with trite memes and baby photos." No, John the Baptist says, "If you have two cloaks, give one to somebody who has none. Do the same with your food. Basically, make some room in your heart to have compassion for others." I guess that's still the message today. If we really want to experience Christ alive in our world, we need to change our perspectives and priorities. Make room in our hearts for a whole lot of love.

⁂

Mmm, the Smell of Manual Labor

IN 1972 I WAS A WILY EIGHT-YEAR-OLD WITH A BASEBALL GLOVE HANGING ON THE HANDLEBARS OF MY BICYCLE. I needed to step on a cinder block to actually get on the bike, and my feet barely touched the pedals, but I was proud as punch. Life was pretty good, very nearly a cliché. As a small kid in a small town, I had the privilege of being oblivious to the turmoil going on in the world around me during those years—the war in Vietnam, the fight for racial equality, the Cold War with its nuclear threat, and the leaked Pentagon Papers. My biggest concern was saving enough coins to purchase my next Matchbox car.

Life was considerably harder for my father. He was a young carpenter working long days and late nights to support his wife and four children. I barely saw him. He left each morning long before I rolled out of bed, came home for dinner with the family around 6 PM, and then worked again in the evenings well past my bedtime. But he was my hero, and we had two wonderful, glorious embraces every day. As the clock ticked past 5:30, I would hang out near our back door, waiting impatiently for the sound of his truck in the driveway. When he walked through the door, I'd leap into his strong arms and fill my nose with the smell of sawdust and sweat. Later in the evening, proudly dressed in Green Bay Packers pajamas, I'd make a bare-footed dash across the yard to Dad's workshop to say goodnight and get a hug. Again, I'd breathe in the distinct scent of oak or maple or pine blended with human perspiration. This was no store-bought cologne; it was one hundred percent all-natural perfume.

In my mind, this is how love smelled, and this is what men did; they loved their children and they worked hard to support their families. If something was made better, when the kitchen was remodeled or the church was painted, when old cars were fixed or new trees were planted, it was because someone rolled up his sleeves and got to work. Nothing happened by itself. Behind everything that worked were people who worked, people who loved their children and set down tools to give them hugs.

It was in this era, in the tension between down-home values and an increasing awareness of an unjust world, that Pope Paul VI gave us these famous words: "If you want peace, work for justice." This was and remains powerful and sage wisdom. He could have said if you want peace, pray for justice, or promote justice, or pursue justice, or vote for justice, or even fight for justice. All would have been appropriate. But the verb the Holy Father chose was *work*, work for justice.

The word "work" is powerful on three levels: it is active, it is constructive, and it is personal. We can and should pray, promote, pursue, and vote for justice, yes, but it's not enough.

As St. James writes, faith without good works is dead (James 2:14–26). It's empty, meaningless. If we want peace, it is not enough to talk about it. We are called to put our faith into action, to grab hammers and shovels, to put our backs into our labor, and to work to advance justice for all humanity. This is what Christian disciples do—they work.

Second, the word "work" invokes a spirit of being constructive. Almost all public dialog lately is destructive. It tears people down by criticizing, condemning, and complaining. Work, in the tradition of the carpenter's son, is about building something good. If we want peace, we must build justice.

And third, the word "work" makes it personal. Work not only requires something *from* us; it requires something *of* us. We have to give of our own time and energy, of our own selves. "Do you love me?" Jesus asks Peter. "Yes, Lord, you know that I love you." "Then feed my lambs. Tend my sheep," Jesus says. Go out in the world and get to work. In a representative democracy, we too easily buy into the illusion that we can change the world by electing others to bring about justice without ever having to roll up our own sleeves or get our hands dirty. But we cannot be disciples by proxy. We have to do it ourselves.

Not all of us can work for justice. The sick, the aging, those with mental illness, victims of abuse and human trafficking, children, the preborn...these people are unable to work for justice, so they need us to work all the harder on their behalf. Yes, we should pray for them, vote for them, and even fight for them. But mostly, they need us to work for them. To work in a way that is active, constructive, and personal.

Christianity is a working faith. Whatever you *do* for the least, Jesus said, you *do* for me. Do the hard work. Break yourself open and pour yourself out in the name of justice for others. That's what love looks like. *Do* this in memory of me.

The world may be a complex and dangerous place, but that's not new. It wasn't new in 1971 and it wasn't new in 1941, or in 1861 or in the year 31. But if anything is going to be made better, it's because someone is willing to do the work to make it better. Discipleship is a scent people should be able to smell on us, and it should smell one hundred percent all natural as it drips off our brows and seeps from our pores. If you want peace, WORK for justice.

∽⦚⦚⦚⦚⦚⦚⦚⦚⦚⦚⦚⦚·⦚⦚⦚⦚⦚⦚⦚⦚⦚⦚⦚⦚∾

Mary

MARY PLOPPED HERSELF DOWN UNDER AN OLIVE TREE AND TOOK A LOAD OFF. The water jar she was carrying from the well seemed especially heavy this morning. Everything seemed especially heavy this morning. She hadn't slept well. Ugh, the wedding plans were starting to get stressful and Joey (he hated it when she called him that) just didn't seem to engage. He was no help. Is this what marriage was going to be like, leaving her to deal with everything while he's off at his "job" all day? What if she wants to get her own job? He won't even discuss it. That's all she's asking for, to just have a conversation. Is that too much to ask? Doesn't she have a right to dream too?

Two moons ago she saw some really cute embroidered foot-washing towels on Pinterest, which motivated her to practice embroidering *Mrs. Joseph of Nazereth* on every spare cloth around the house. So far, she had practiced with Gothic, Hebrew, and Standard fonts, and she really wanted to try New Roman, but it felt rather sinful, so she wouldn't do it. If she got really good, maybe she could go down to Jerusalem and sell commemorative foot-washing towels to pilgrims outside the temple. It would probably never happen, but at least she could dream, couldn't she? But whenever she brought it up to Joey he rolled his eyes and told her to be practical. The whole thing hung like a dark cloud over their relationship lately.

When she looked up, it wasn't a dark cloud blocking the sun but an imposing figure casting a heavy shadow. It had appeared out of nowhere while she was lost in thought. She recoiled, startled and frightened. With its back to the bright sun, the figure seemed to radiate light as Mary's eyes adjusted. It held a scroll in one hand and what appeared to be some sort of horn in the other. And were those...wings?

"Who are...what do you want?" Mary stammered.

"I'm Gab..." The figure's voice cracked nervously, and he paused to clear his throat before beginning again. "I'm Gabriel, Archangel of the Lord Most High, God of Abraham, Isaac, Moses, and David. I've come with a message for you." His voice had a surprisingly prepubescent quality that didn't match his physical stature.

"Wow. I've heard some pick-up lines before, but a messenger from God?! That's rich."

"Seriously," the angel said. He knew he had a credibility problem. It was suggested during his last performance review that he should start carrying a sword like the Archangel Michael. No one questioned Michael. But Gabriel wasn't into that whole macho image thing. Besides, the weight and leverage of that sword was a sure recipe for carpel tunnel syndrome. Let's see how tough Michael is in another five hundred years when he can't even hold his own hairbrush.

"Well, let's hear it," Mary said. "What's the message?"

"You are to have a child!" Gabriel proclaimed and then put the horn to his mouth and blared a fanfare.

Of course, this made Mary very nervous. Her eyes grew big and she embraced her knees, pulling them close to her chest. "I have early onset leprosy," she blurted. She didn't really, but it's what her grandmother had told her to say if she was being bothered by a man who wouldn't leave her alone. Bubbe had said that no man would dare lay a finger on a woman with leprosy.

"You do not have leprosy," Gabriel sighed. He sat down on the ground facing her. "Look, I understand you're nervous, but here's the deal: I really am an angel. Look, wings and everything." Then he pulled a business card and photo ID with a watermark and hologram from his satchel and handed it to her. It all seemed to be legit. "I was sent to tell you that you are already pregnant with God's child. You will have a son and name him Jesus, and he's going to be the Savior of the world."

"Why me?"

"Because you're a good egg, Mary. You're sweet and kind and generous and compassionate. You have a pure heart and a loving soul. There is no one better to bring God's son to life in this world and to raise him with the loving centeredness to be true to his mission. You were made for this."

It all sounded so odd, yet somehow it felt honest and natural. The rest of the world might think this whole thing is really weird, but something stirred deep within her. For the longest time they sat in silence. Finally, she looked at Gabriel and said, "OK."

"OK what?"

"OK, I'll do it. I'll have God's son."

"Really? Just like that? I mean...don't you need time to think it over?"

"Nope. If it's what God wants, then it's what I want."

Gabriel had not expected it to be this easy. He had anticipated objections. On the whiteboard back at the office, he had mapped out a comprehensive engagement strategy that accounted for every possible argument: 1) not enough time; 2) not in my plans; 3) social risk; 4) can't afford it; 5) interferes with my dreams; 6) what would Joseph say; 7) not worthy; and 8) maybe later but not at this time. He had invested weeks in crafting his responses and counterpoints. The one thing for which he hadn't planned was that Mary would simply agree. Frankly, it annoyed him a little.

"Well, let me walk you through the proposal so you fully understand what's involved," he said.

"That's not necessary," she replied. "I'm in."

He looked at her, not knowing what to say. A strange cascade of questions washed over him. Who *is* this person? Does she understand what this means? Why would anyone sign up for this without reading the fine print? Did God know she would say yes so easily? And if so, why did God let him pour so much work into preparing for this meeting?

"But I've prepared this whole PowerPoint presentation with infographics and data charts. I even have spreadsheets that organize a global needs analysis. Don't you want to at least review the materials?"

"Not especially."

And thus it came to pass. The greatest gifts to humanity come by way of blind faith and strong belief.

⊸᠀᠀᠀᠀᠀᠀᠀᠀᠀᠀᠀᠀·᠀᠀᠀᠀᠀᠀᠀᠀᠀᠀᠀⊷

Island of Misfit Toys

ONE OF CHILDHOOD'S MOST ENDEARING IMAGES, AT LEAST FOR ME, IS THE ISLAND OF MISFIT TOYS ON THE *RUDOLPH THE RED-NOSED REINDEER* CHRISTMAS TELEVISION SPECIAL. More than just a children's tale, it is about the experience of being broken in some way, of being imperfect and discovering redeeming qualities in those imperfections. In other words, the story is about each of us on our human journey. Whether it's Rudolph, who is mocked for his crimson beak, Hermey the elf, who would rather be a dentist than make toys, or the hapless prospector Yukon Cornelius looking for the wrong stuff in the wrong places, all the main characters are broken. They stumble upon an island populated by toys no child would want, such as an elephant with spots and a train with square wheels. The ultimate point is that all are lovable, all have value, regardless of oddities and nonconformities.

The concept of incarnation—the idea that God becomes one with humanity—acknowledges that our earth is, in fact, an island of misfit toys. At times, each of us has felt broken in some way, discouraged, or ostracized. We bumble like the Abominable Snowmonster (nicknamed "Bumble") in the Rudolph story, sometimes living in our own anger and fear. We feel misunderstood or misplaced, like Hermey, yearning to share our true passions and talents with the world. Or, like the cowboy who rides an ostrich, we're just convinced we can't be lovable unless we conform to the expectations of others.

Ironically, we exhaust much of our lives in pursuit of perfection rather than in celebration of our uniqueness and differences. Many of us aspire to a 1950s-sitcom image of a nuclear family joyfully singing around a piano next to a toasty fire, and we picture success as the image of beautiful people in snappy fashions sipping pinot grigio on a beach-house veranda. Everyone is happy. No one is stressed or exhausted. The problem is that no one really lives this way. We all have storybook moments in our lives, but most of our days are spent paying bills and cleaning toilets. We struggle to make ends meet; we wrestle tirelessly with voices of doubt, criticism, and judgment; and we carry scars from past pain, abuse, or loss.

The Christian nativity story provides a far better image of incarnation. It is the story of a frightened, unwed teenage girl giving birth in a barn in the middle of a cold night. No matter how much we try to romanticize it, the nativity stable filled with filthy sheep and smelly shepherds is an island of misfit toys. And there, in the midst of disheveled, broken, exhausted imperfection, we find our redemption.

God's love is unconditional not because we are perfect but rather because we are not. We may have square wheels on our caboose, but that doesn't distract from our intrinsic human value! For many who suffer in grief, loneliness, poverty, imprisonment, or homelessness, the whole notion of incarnation ought to bring a warm embrace, an experience of personal love, and an affirmation of personal value. Instead, because of so many false images of perfect families singing carols in perfect harmony, it becomes a very painful reminder of just how imperfect we are. Many for whom incarnation is most intended dread Christmas because they simply cannot live up to the expectations.

As for those of us whose wounds have healed, who aren't carrying heavy burdens, and who do live in homes that resonate abounding love, do we love with God's love, reaching beyond the brokenness of others to value and cherish every person? Or do we limit our love only to those who conform to our images and expectations? Acknowledging our place on this island of misfits, how can we reach out to those with red noses or square wheels?

Bare Butts on Cold Stone

AUGUSTE RODIN'S FAMOUS SCULPTURE *THE THINKER* DEPICTS A MAN WITH HIS CHIN RESTING ON ONE HAND. At first glance, it looks serene, and we're apt to think, "You know, we need more of that in this world." The viewer gets the sense of an intelligent man at rest who has gone inward. You barely notice he is nude and sitting on a rock, hardly a comfortable way to go. Although the statue has an ancient Greek vibe, it was actually commissioned in 1880. Certainly, Rodin knew about chairs and trousers!

I know a little about sitting on rocks and thinking. When backpacking in the mountains, the choice is to sit on whatever rock can be found, sit on the ground, or remain standing for several days. So, having spent many hours sitting on rocks under blue skies while contemplating the meaning of life, I feel a certain kinship with *The Thinker*. But there is something you need to know about rocks—they're very hard, even harder than church pews. Also, they tend to be uncomfortably jagged or rounded. And they're typically strewn with dirt and bugs. So I recommend keeping your pants on for whatever protection and thin cushion they provide.

But maybe that's Rodin's insight. Perhaps the process of true introspection—a deep dive into one's own soul, where the false divide between human experience and divine truth dissolves into the holy oneness of creation—maybe that's supposed to feel uncomfortable. Maybe it's supposed to challenge us, leave us exposed, and reveal our vulnerability. I remind you, however, that *The Thinker* is an artistic expression, not a literal depiction. There is no need to streak through a briar patch in search for God. (But if that is your thing, please use plenty of sunscreen and mosquito repellent. Even vulnerability has its limits.)

There is a strong spiritual benefit to venturing beyond stained glass to a place where our souls stir into the cosmos. The wilderness has a way of grounding us while also inspiring us. It's simultaneously uncomfortable and transcendent. Where did Jesus go when he needed to discern his mission? The desert. And where did he go to pray? The mountain. And where does John the Baptist reach us? While calling from the wilderness. Let's not miss the consistent spiritual metaphor. The wilderness refers to a place beyond our own comfort zones where we face our vulnerabilities and encounter our true nature.

There's certainly nothing wrong with being comfortable, but true spiritual growth happens beyond the edges of our comfort zones. I'll offer a couple examples from my own experience. When we first started StreetLights Outreach, I was pushed way beyond my personal happy places. Sitting on a street corner at midnight in an at-risk neighborhood was a real wilderness. But the voice called to me from there. And from that corner I've learned so much about myself, humanity, and God. Another wilderness for me is fatherhood. Being strong while my heart is melting, realizing everything I say and do is role modeling, recognizing that these living, breathing expressions of God are entrusted to me to steward but not to shape, it's all a very vulnerable place to be. But a voice calls to me from the wilderness of parenthood.

It is good to have spiritual practices that give us comfort. We need them. But we're invited to sit on the rock and dive deeply into our own spiritual wilderness as well. What is beyond the boundary of our spiritual comfort zones? Where in our personal wilderness do we hear the voice crying out to us? It's different for everyone. It might be forgiveness of self or another for a past wrong, or reconciliation of a relationship. It might be a social justice call, or a call to open your mind to new ideas and perspectives. It might be as simple as a book you're being led to read or as complex as learning self-love.

The voice cries out, but if we curl up in the safety our own comfort zones and pull a blanket of security over our heads, we might not hear it. We need to step out—step out into our wilderness.

The Wilderness at the Top of the Stairs

JORGE AND MELIA MOVED INTO THE HOUSE OF THEIR DREAMS ON A TREE-LINED STREET ONE BLOCK OFF THE LAKE. This is where they would raise a son and a daughter, helping them with homework at the kitchen table and playing kickball beneath the maples in the yard. And such is the way life would go—first steps, first days of school, first Communions, first dates. It was almost a poem. Almost.

If you walked up the stairs, listening to the old wood creak beneath your steps, and proceeded down the hallway on the second floor, you'd feel an uneasy sense of ominous caution. At the end of the hall an old door with a "Do NOT Enter" sign remained closed. Those who bravely reached for the knob would feel their hearts beat a little faster. The hairs on their arms would stand on end. Sometimes there was a stench. Jorge called this closed-off room the *dangerous lair of the unpredictable beast*; Melia called it the *wilderness where angels fear to tread*. This was the bedroom of their teenage son, Sergio. Standing on the threshold, both Jorge and Melia proclaimed the coming of the Savior: "Oh Lord, it's going to take one far greater than us to raise this kid."

Parenthood is a wilderness requiring great courage, as is marriage, divorce, a new job, the loss of a job, and everything else that leaves us vulnerable. A well-lived life will venture into many wildernesses, some we choose and some that choose us. These are the experiences that challenge us, make our palms sweat, keep us awake at night, and force us to come to terms with our own identities.

It's a popular motif throughout Scripture. Abraham was a nomad in the desert. Moses was exiled into the wilderness where he discovered his true purpose in life, and the Jews wandered in the desert where they reclaimed their identity. Writing from exile in Babylon, Isaiah says, "A voice proclaims: In the wilderness prepare the way of the Lord." John the Baptist preaches in the wilderness, Jesus is born in the wilderness, and he returns to the wilderness, where he faces the temptations and comes to terms with his identity.

Like Jorge and Melia, spiritually centered parents thank their children for leading, sometimes forcing, them into the wilderness. The stories passed to them from their parents, the same stories they pass to their children, as has been the tradition through the generations, have so many references to the desert, the mountain, and the wilderness that we need to pay attention and ask ourselves what that's about. What does it mean?

To the ancients, "wilderness" referred to any place where there was no roof, no shelter, no security. As pilgrims journeying through a lifetime, we are invited to venture with John the Baptist into the wilderness, beyond our own security and comfort. We're called to stretch ourselves beyond our walls of prejudice and intolerance, to walk out from beneath the protective roof of self-righteousness and judgment, and to journey into the wilderness of forgiveness, mercy, and unconditional love. It's a scary door we would often prefer to leave closed.

If God is to come to life within us, if Christ himself is to be born in the mangers of our own hearts, then we need to get busy and prepare the way through the wilderness within. We need to fill in the valleys, level the mountains, break down the walls, and crumble the ceilings. What anxieties hold us back? What fears leave us locked out of our own fullness?

Part Two

CELEBRATION

Bare Feet
on Vinyl Floors

ARRIVING HOME FROM WORK WHEN ALEX WAS THREE YEARS OLD WAS AN AMAZING TREAT. In retrospect, even saying it sounds ridiculous. Who looks forward to dealing with a three-year-old after a long day of coping with corporate politics? Some might suggest, with tongues only partially lodged in cheeks, it was just more of the same. But Alex had a way of exploding with joy when I walked through the door. It was ridiculously contagious. No matter how difficult or stressful a day may have been, Alex erased the clouds and beamed sunshine. As soon as I stepped across the threshold, he would come running, his small bare feet slapping the vinyl floor as he raced across the kitchen, and with arms extended he'd leap up and give me a great big welcome home.

One day, when feeling particularly worn down—the type of day where you ask yourself why you even bother—I opened the door and sure enough, my answer came in the swift patter of Alex flying through the house. I scooped him into my arms, gazed into his eyes—eyes as wide as the Montana sky—and said, "I love you, Alex. I love you as much as one person can possibly love another."

With a bright face as full of delight as a Sunday morning in May, Alex looked back into my eyes and said, "I'm going to hit you, Daddy."

I laughed until my eyes watered. Alex was teasing, of course. He was joy-filled and held no malice; he was merely expressing his good-natured way of throwing me off balance, a personality cornerstone he has maintained into adulthood. On that particular evening, with my spirit crawling in the back alley of defeat, Alex brought me back to life. In that moment I discovered how love could, indeed, expand in all directions. I learned we're able to touch heaven from earth just as surely as Christ touched earth from heaven. That's the glory of love, right there: an ordinary moment in time that's made extraordinary by the love shared between two people.

When Jesus turns water into wine, he takes something very ordinary—water—and he makes it extraordinary—wine. And he does it at a wedding—a celebration of love so divine that it empowers two ordinary people to become co-creators with God. In other words, when we drink in the awesome miracle of ever-expanding love, this rather mundane, ordinary life takes on a whole new rich and vibrant flavor. We're suddenly able to taste sacredness in laughter. We're aware that a meal shared with others is divine. The hug of a child, the embrace of a grandparent, and the smile of a stranger become encounters with the very real presence of a very real Christ. Water becomes wine. Wine becomes the blood of Christ. And Christ becomes you and me. The ordinary becomes extraordinary.

Unfortunately, the opposite is also true. When we crowd out or close off the miracle of infinite love, we miss the divine poetry of life. God and humanity become distant and separate. Relationships go flat and stale. The water never becomes wine. We don't see the blood of Christ in the cup.

Perhaps the stone jars of our culture sit empty far too often, void of Christ's selfless compassion. Have we crowded out and grown increasingly blind to the divine presence of God's love in our world? It's as though the wedding is winding down and the evening is getting dull. The wine—the spirit—has gone dry. We have everything, yet our children are bored. People strap parachutes to themselves and jump off buildings to give themselves thrills. We spend dead-time hours watching shows like *The Bachelor*, which means we are so bored we watch someone else's fabricated reality. It's actually quite bizarre. We are stressed out, over tired, and weary with anxiety. We keep chasing the next artificial high, hoping we can feel joy again. With designer handbags, bigger boats, more exotic vacations, and faster downloads, we're able to add artificial flavors and sweeteners and perhaps a few bubbles to the drab water of life. We can turn the water into Diet Coke, but we can't turn it into the fruit of the vine. Only the love of Christ can do that. Only the love of God can make the ordinary extraordinary.

This is something God has done throughout time. An old, anonymous nomad named Abraham. The abandoned slave infant called Moses. The smallest, youngest, most unlikely son of a sheep herder who was called David. A poor peasant girl from the backwoods named Mary and her seemingly illegitimate son, Jesus. A ragamuffin fisherman called Peter. A murderous Pharisee named Paul. Extremely ordinary people made extraordinary by the love of God.

In turning water into wine, Jesus invites us to open our eyes to the divine love of God...in ourselves and in everyone else. The lifeblood of the party is right here, right now before our very eyes. But it's not where you expect it to be. The ordinary is extraordinary. Can you see it...in yourself, in your neighbor, in every human being created in God's own image and likeness?

XXXL Gratitude with Matching Socks

JEFFERY DIDN'T SPEAK. Not a whisper. He didn't even attempt to move his lips. He just offered a subtle nod. For most of his life, his size had spoken for him, often saying far more than he would have liked. It spoke with a volume that frightened children and a tone that intimidated men. So he had learned to keep his distance. Perhaps, he reasoned, he wouldn't appear so freakishly large if he wasn't next to anyone else, if there was no comparative reference for the length of his bones, the size of his head, or the span of his hands. People were friendlier if they weren't up close; they weren't as uncomfortable, and they didn't regard him as an oddity.

He was brought to the shelter by the police officers responding to calls by concerned passers-by who had seen Jeffery convulsing on the sidewalk. Some assumed he had overdosed. Others concluded he was dying. In reality, Jeffery suffered from seizures. On this particular night, he had a couple particularly bad episodes, so bad that he had lost all control of his bodily functions. As he silently hunched in the shelter's entry, he looked like a man who would prefer to be invisible, with shoulders drooped, eyes fixed on the floor, hands buried in the pockets of his soiled jeans, and knees ready to buckle with the next breath. Using a back corridor, we quietly rushed him to the front of the line for the shelter's lone shower, and because all his clothing was ruined and had to be destroyed, I dove into the storage rooms to find suitable attire for this unusually large man.

Shuffling through shelves in search of decent clothes in exceptional sizes, I was suddenly struck by Jeffery's sacred and vulnerable humanity. He was not the sort of person others typically looked upon with empathy and mercy. Upon first encounter, one would conclude this man could handle his own business; certainly, he could carry whatever burden God places upon those ox-like shoulders. Yet, just minutes earlier, I had felt the weightlessness of complete surrender in his handshake. I had read in his face a story of defeat and brokenness. It felt overwhelming. A lump formed in my throat, a tear in the corner of my eye. My own knees buckled and I slid to the floor where I sat and wept. I cried for all the hurting people I had looked past. I cried for the lonely and forgotten. I cried for Jeffery. And I cried for the emptiness within myself that he had managed to open and expose.

The task at hand was not a matter of function; it was a mission of mercy. I wasn't simply finding clothes for a stranger; I was finding myself. I found myself driven to restore this man's value and dignity. I found myself inspired by the shelter staff, who cared so deeply for this man who had just walked through their door. And I found myself filled with deep gratitude for all the anonymous people who had donated brand-new underwear and socks in XXXL sizes. I found jeans, t-shirts, a warm flannel shirt, and a set of sweats for him to sleep in. I even found a pair of size fourteen shoes!

I gathered all these things and set them on a chair outside the shower. When Jeffery emerged, he was renewed. This man who less than an hour earlier had been broken and compromised more than anyone I had ever met—homeless, naked, suffering, alone—was renewed, refreshed, and restored.

This is what mercy does—it transforms both the one who receives it and the one who gives it. It opens our hearts to the sacredness of one another; it allows us to enter each other's stories. Mercy removes the filters of bias and ego, bringing us eye-to-eye and heart-to-heart with God.

⤳ϗϗϗϗϗϗϗϗϗϗϗϗϗ · ϧϧϧϧϧϧϧϧϧϧϧϧϧ ⤲

Dandelion Peace Talks of 2016

SERENA POURED WINE FOR THE NEIGHBORS GATHERED ON THE PATIO. She and Nigel had invited Leonard and Eva, next-door neighbors to the east, and Sullivan "Sully" Jones, who lived next-door to the west. Sully's wife, Rose, had lost a battle with cancer the previous autumn, and this was the first time the neighbors had all gotten together in nearly a year.

Sully was a self-described Dodge Ram Lutheran who frequently commented on the "rice rockets" parked in the driveway of those bead-bangers, his favorite nickname for Catholics, specifically Leonard and Eva. Leonard was an English teacher at the local high school and coached the forensics team. Sully thought he was a bit of an elitist. Leonard thought Sully was a bit of a redneck. But Leonard and Sully set all that aside to agree on one thing: that dandelions sprouted through the earth's crust from the depths of hell. They both went to great lengths to rid their lawns of the yellow plague. And both were adamant that Serena and Nigel were unacceptably negligent in this regard. In planning the evening, Serena and Nigel had secretly referred to it as the Dandelion Peace Talks of 2016.

Serena had grown weary of the persistent badgering from both neighbors. At first, she dismissed it, claiming dandelions are God's way of spreading joy. She recalled picking bouquets for her mother, and the first time one of her own sons presented her with a fistful of dandelions, her heart melted all over her Birkenstocks. She put the bouquet in a glass with water and perched it in the window above the kitchen sink, just as her mother had. Warm memories aside, there was no way she was allowing anyone to spread chemicals of any sort on the lawn where her children played. For his part, Nigel consistently told Leonard and Sully, "We're raising boys, not grass."

When exactly does a weed become a weed? My college botany professor insisted there are no weeds in nature, just plants growing where we decide we don't want them. He also ate pine cones, so we can take it for what it's worth. I had one neighbor who would crawl across her lawn and uproot every dandelion one by one, and another neighbor who collected them and made dandelion wine. So what makes one plant a weed and another plant wheat?

In the context of a garden or a field, weeds hog the nutrients from the soil only for themselves and bear no fruit, making them the organized criminals of the botanical world. Wheat, however, grows to ultimately nourish others, like special education teachers and mothers. Fair enough. But how much of this is a matter of perspective? For nearly two hundred years in America, tomatoes were considered vulgar and obscene, even while they flavored the cuisine of Spain and Italy. It wasn't until the early twentieth century that Americans accepted tomatoes as cultural wheat, not cultural weeds. Likewise, many people consider chamomile to be a weed; yes, the same chamomile that makes the tea used to relieve stress and cure sleep deprivation.

The ideas of redemption and resurrection require us to take a second look at the concept of weeds. Who is to say that something or someone has no purpose or value? I suppose St. Paul and St. Francis would have been considered to be weeds before their conversions, as was the good Samaritan by the people of his time, and sadly, many immigrants and refugees in our time.

What happens when we examine the garden of our own lives? Most of us are part weed and part wheat. At our best, we take in the sunshine, rain, and nutrients we are given, and we grow to serve and nourish the lives of others. This is how the ecosystem of God's creation seems designed to work. But we all have not-so-good days as well, days when we're not at our best, when our pride and self-centeredness suck the energy out of the room. These are our weed days, but, thankfully, such is not a permanent state. Each new day is a chance at redemption, each morning brings a new resurrection.

The neighbors raised their glasses and the evening sun illuminated the golden color of the wine, which Nigel had made himself and aged in his basement. He offered a toast, "To Rose, whose generous love spread like dandelions and now brightens our neighborhood."

Star Wars Monopoly
Makes Me Cry

SCHEDULES BEING WHAT THEY WERE, IT TOOK UNTIL THE WEEKEND OF EPIPHANY BEFORE WE WERE FINALLY ABLE TO GATHER OUR WHOLE FAMILY TO CELEBRATE CHRISTMAS, or, as my mother describes it, until we had all the gingerbread men back in the cookie jar. Mom's a poet. Jacob and his wife, Jenny, made it up from Omaha—he was wearing a cowboy hat, which, if you knew Jacob, equates to ten gallons of irony. Alex and Adam were home from college along with their girlfriends, so we actually had as many women as men around our table, which heightened manners and sophistication. Our sons might be well-educated adult men, but in certain areas, such as Legos, Star Wars, and armpit farts, they are twelve-year-old boys.

This might come as a surprise. Since all three of our sons have my genetic material, you probably think it was a subdued weekend, with everyone sitting around quietly, sipping warm milk, and reading books about Jesus. But I'd remind you that the boys also have Michelle's genetics, so they can get a little rowdy. The Star Wars Monopoly games were particularly rambunctious as the women formed an alliance to defeat the men, and all three of my sons conspired to prevent me from obtaining all the orange properties. Regardless of the outcome, I felt I won simply because they let me have the Han Solo game token.

There were several times over the extended weekend when we were gathered around the table laughing so hard our eyes were filled with tears and we could hardly breathe. At moments like these, immersed in so much love and over-whelmed with so much gratitude, you realize that God is as close as your own heart, and heaven is as near as the person next to you.

I had felt this same way six months earlier, when I gathered with my mother, my brother Charles, and my sisters Mary and Carol on the night Dad died. There, too, our eyes filled with tears and we could hardly breathe. But immersed in love and overwhelmed with gratitude, we knew God was as close as our own hearts and heaven as near as one another. In both the height of joy and depth of sorrow, and in all experiences between, God is immediately present to us, around us, among us, and within us. We recalled how some of our best memories as children were when we gathered around the table and played Monopoly with Dad. It was at this point that Mom revealed a secret she had kept for over forty years: Dad hated Monopoly. He played it with us endlessly simply because we all enjoyed spending the time together so much. This caused us to laugh and cry even harder. What a gift! What an example!

Too often we let self-interest divide rather than unify. Instead of entering into the wonder and awe of spirit, which enters us with each breath, we think in dimensional or even oppositional terms: Me here, God there; earth now, heaven later. We live like Samuel, who hears himself being called but runs to Eli because it never occurs to him that God is right there in the room with him. Sometimes it seems as though we've dismissed the whole idea of incarnation and resurrec-tion—God with us and among us—the idea of Eucharist—God for us and within us—and Pentecost—God upon us.

Paul tries to explain it when he emphatically appeals through his First Letter to the Corinthians (6:15), "Do you not know that your bodies are members of Christ?" You can almost hear the frustration in his voice. Don't you get it?! You are not separate from God! You and I are not separate from each other! We are *one*! He goes on, but perhaps it helps to paraphrase: You don't have to wait until after you die to be one with God. The Holy Spirit is within you now. Here. In this body. Heaven is not separate from earth. God is not separate from humanity. God is as close as your own heart, and heaven is as near as the person next to you. It's a wonderful, comforting, and inspiring truth. To enter it, we only need to release ourselves from the grip of ego, the clenches of separateness.

The most powerful life insight I received from my father, and hopefully have been able to pass to my sons, is to not care about the game itself. *What* we're doing is not nearly as important as *why* we're doing it. And that *why* is pretty straightforward—to love one another. This is how we enter the sacred Oneness of Christ, the immediacy of heaven. God is right here. The gates of heaven are right now. And we're all welcome to open our hearts and come on in.

I'm King
of the World!

IT FELT GOOD TO GET BACK ON A MOUNTAIN. I needed it; Alex needed it. It had been seven years since I had strapped up a backpack and set a boot down in the Rockies. Alex had recently turned fourteen, spurring within me this fatherly intuition to expose him to a hard-fought lesson in self-reliance and perseverance. He had reached the age where he was pretty sure he had life figured out and equally confident that I did not. So off we went. We headed to upper Savage Lake, a manly sounding destination at an oxygen-depleted altitude of 11,200 feet in Colorado's Holy Cross Wilderness.

My plan was simple. It was the same plan that had worked brilliantly with his brother seven years prior. About halfway up the mountain, Alex would start to break, beaten down, fatigued, and short of breath. I'd encourage him on. He'd dig in, simultaneously discovering a new depth of humility and a new height of personal triumph with each step. He'd regain respect for his father and no longer think I was, in his words, lame. And by the end of the trek the boy would be a man, broken and resurrected, having opened a deep and sacred place within himself. That's how I imagined it.

The mid-afternoon sun was direct and hot when we reached our destination after a tremendously arduous and taxing climb. I was spent. We had been hiking up a steep, rocky slope since early morning and I was exhausted, craving ibuprofen. Alex was coming up the trail behind me, so I waited with anticipation for the moment when he would collapse in humble relief. We would have a moment of shared triumph, father and son, bonded in mutual respect.

Instead, he dropped his pack, ran right past me, scurried up a large bolder the size of a small house, and proclaimed himself KING OF THE WORLD! So much for life lessons. "This is going to be a three-day par-tay!" he declared. Then turning to me he asked, "What do you want to do now?" I told him to start looking for downed firewood. He ran instead to a pile of residual snowcap, packed his first-ever July snowball, and hurled it at me. Not knowing the Colorado statutes governing corporal punishment, I refrained from striking the child, as though I could have caught him had I tried.

Life seldom follows the scripts I write. Instead, it takes wild twists and turns more marvelous than can be woven by the rickety loom of my imagination. Alex wasn't broken at all. He was alive and invigorated, with an electric smile so radiant I could only respond with admiring awe. I had hoped he would get a glimpse into his own soul, but it was I who was provided the sacred glimpse into his soul, and it was brilliant! He simply exploded with infinite love and joy. In perfect harmony with the glory of creation, the gifted became the giver, and I, the blessed recipient.

Pain is inevitable along life's journey, and it's not as though Alex made the climb without hurt and fatigue. "It was the hardest thing I've ever done," he would tell me later. This admission satisfied me in an oddly comforting but guilt-ridden way. I was glad to learn he had been tested, and I was impressed by how he persevered. The pain and exhaustion had left him unfazed. His spirit and disposition were undaunted. Was it because he was fourteen and lacked the life experience to know how to gripe, whine, and feel sorry for himself? Or was it because I was forty-five and lacked the wisdom not to? We all know the answer so there's no point in pursuing the question further.

Ultimately, I go backpacking to personally encounter God in the mountain solitude. On this trek into the Holy Cross Wilderness, it was I who was broken and resurrected. I am still and always shall be much more a student than a teacher.

God Plays a Purple Banjo

GOD DECIDED TO GET AN INTERN, SO HE SUMMONED GABRIEL. "Gabs," he said, "I need you to help me find an intern, someone who can handle the light work around here."

Gabriel was confused. Things seemed to be in order and running smoothly; prayers were being answered in a timely and orderly fashion, even with the huge increase in volume since the proliferation of casinos and lotteries. The training program on earth was admittedly in a bit of disarray, though. Still, was an intern with no real experience the answer? "Are you sure?" he asked. "What's driving this?"

"Well, a few things," said God as he leaned back, rubbed his beard contemplatively like some sort of philosopher, and stared skyward. "First, I think we need help in the Joy Department. We just can't seem to keep up with demand. Second, it's becoming increasingly difficult to squeeze a Sabbath in. I'd like a little more time for R&R if retirement isn't in the stars for me. I need to unplug and rejuvenate the spirit. And third, frankly, I think we could all benefit from some more youthful energy around here."

That last part stung a bit. Was it a slight to the angels? Did God think his team had lost a step? He tensed and leaned in, but then thought better of it. Sighing, he slumped into his chair, resigned to God's plan. Every time God decided to add staff, it meant more work for Gabriel. "So, what do you have in mind?"

"We need someone who is exuberant and full of life, someone who explodes with joy and is delighted to be alive." God had been thinking about this for a while. He clearly had a vision, as he did with pretty much everything except the walrus. God still took a little ribbing about the way that thing was thrown together. He continued, "But it needs to be authentic joy, the kind that resonates from within. It can't be the type of joy that's expressed in response to external things like winning a basketball game, or conditional joy like a bride on her wedding day."

Gabriel fixed his eyes to prevent them from rolling. This felt like the time God asked him to help Noah locate two albino squirrels and then complained they weren't white enough. "All right," he nodded as patiently as he could. "How is authentic joy different from responsive joy or conditional joy?"

"Great question," God chirped as though he had been anticipating it. "Authentic joy is an inner disposition that explodes into the world for no other reason than an exuberance for life. Responsive joy and conditional joy are great, but they're contingent on external things outside of the soul."

Gabriel stared for a long moment before speaking, hoping God caught the subtlety in his tone. "So...you want me to find someone who is joyful for no reason?"

"Yes, Gabs! Exactly!" God was getting excited. "Pure spiritual joy is the type that can only be of God and from God. It's beyond personal happiness. It's my own divine presence seeded in a person's soul and radiating into the world. That's what we need. Find someone with that fire."

"I, uhmm, I don't know if you've created a lot of people like that."

"I've created every person like that! They just have a way of draining it out of one another. We need to find someone who still has it."

Silence fell over the room. Gabriel couldn't get the lyrics to the song "Joy to the World" out of his head, which led to the Three Dog Night version: *Joy to the fishes in the deep blue sea, joy to you and me...* Then, for no apparent reason, the "Hold On" lyrics from the band Triumph jumped to mind: *Music holds the secret, to know it can make you whole; it's not just a game of notes, it's the sound inside your soul...*

That's it! Music! He jumped from his chair and raised both arms into the air. "What about the kid who plays the purple banjo?!"

"Adam?" God knew right away who he was talking about. Adam was a three-year-old kid who jumped down from his booster chair after dinner every evening, grabbed a purple toy banjo, and ran around the house singing and dancing with unrestrained glee. For no reason. Every day.

"Yes!" exclaimed Gabriel. "Adam! He even has the perfect name for it—the first person created directly by you in your own image and likeness. He is God's presence in the world. His joy is your joy!"

"I like it," said God. Then he corrected himself. "No, I love it! A three-year-old kid with a purple banjo doing my work in the world. It's perfect! Pure joy."

⤛𝄢𝄢𝄢𝄢𝄢𝄢𝄢𝄢𝄢𝄢𝄢𝄢𝄢·𝄢𝄢𝄢𝄢𝄢𝄢𝄢𝄢𝄢𝄢𝄢𝄢𝄢⤜

Thanks for the Burger, Reg

MR. EISENMAN STOOD IN FRONT OF HIS CLASS OF TRIGONOM-ETRY STUDENTS AND TOOK A DEEP BREATH. As he exhaled, his shoulders drooped. These kids just didn't care. Sputnik had beeped its way around earth's orbit just months before, but all these boys thought about was cars and girls. He decided to give it one more try. "Look," he said as he pointed his chalk in the direction of one young man in particular, "we live in 1957. We don't have the luxury of sloth. The Russians are winning space and all you care about is the grease in your hair." The boys wouldn't even give him the satisfaction of shifting in their seats, further fueling his outrage. "You need to knuckle under and learn these equations. Your nation needs you to apply yourselves or we'll all fall under the rule of those godless communists. Is that what you want? There'll be no more rock-n-roll when that day hits, I can tell you that right now. Your laziness is un-American! Now shape up and pay attention or you'll end up being ditch diggers for the rest of your life!"

Sitting two-thirds of the way back in the room, Ronnie leaned forward and raised his hand. He had heard this lecture once too often. "Excuse me, Mr. Eisenman. I have a question." Ronnie had grown up on a dairy farm and while it was true he'd rather wax his car than learn about cosines, he most certainly was not lazy. "Can you explain why it's un-American to be a ditch digger? I mean, let's say we do launch a rocket into space. All that launching equipment needs to be anchored on the earth. Who's going to dig the foundations and pour the concrete? What makes you think ditch diggers aren't valuable members of society?"

Without realizing it, Ronnie was invoking an old proverb: when you drink water, remember the one who dug the well. It's a good reminder of how interdependent and connected we all are. Even the simplest activities, like drinking a glass of tap water, are made possible through the talents and work of people we will never meet. This does not just include the well drillers, but also the pump manufacturers and installers, the pipe manufacturers, the plumbers, the engineers, and so on.

By remembering those who dig the wells, or farm the fields that give us food, or build the houses we live in, or pave the streets we drive on, we spiritually connect in a way that increases our gratitude and compassion. We belay the ego-serving myth of the self-made man, and we grow in our abiding thankfulness for all people who contribute to our well-being. Hopefully, we also become grateful for the opportunity to contribute to others as well.

I was reminded of this when Reginald stopped by our StreetLights Outreach block party in Whitney Park. Reg spoke softly but had a personality much larger than his height could support. What he lacked vertically he made up for horizontally, which he claimed was needed to carry around such a big heart. Reg was kind, but not complex.

If you met Reg, you'd be taken aback by his showman-like hip-hop presentation. He dressed for our block party in black and gold velvet shorts draping well below his knees, a bright red satin t-shirt that was over-sized even on him, and a red top hat with a wide gold band that matched his sneakers. And bling. He wore lots of over-the-top pawn shop bling. To the unacquainted, it was either intimidating or costume-esque, but to those who knew him, it was just Reg. This was his style and he was going to share it out loud. Very early in a conversation, you would be set at ease by his pleasant, compassionate voice, and after you heard his story, you'd root for the guy. Once you knew Reg, you'd just want him to do well in a world that has been stacked against him his entire life.

It was nice to see Reg again and it was an honor to serve him. I learned he had been working in the kitchen at a small diner where I frequently have lunch. Reg had been serving me the previous several months and I never knew it! Every couple of weeks or so I'd duck in with a colleague and order a cheeseburger with fried onions (yes, I know. Please don't judge me just because my sins are different from yours). In my own task-driven busyness, I had not bothered to think about the person in the back working the grill.

In a flash, I was reminded how often I take people for granted. I had forgotten to remember the one who dug the well. I wished I could go back in time, relive all those lunches, and enjoy them with deep gratitude and appreciation for Reg, the person who had prepared them. Now here he stood, thanking me earnestly for a simple hamburger I had grilled, but not once had I felt sincere appreciation for the meals he had prepared for me.

Every person has a story, and in small, simple ways all those stories intersect with each of ours. How enriched we are for it! When you drink water, remember the one who dug the well.

Part Three

CONSIDERATION

Planting Radishes,
Expecting Daisies

Isadore Schraufnagel, the son of German immigrants and a World War One veteran, was a gentle soul who lived to be ninety-eight years old. For well over sixty of those years, he and his wife farmed down the road from Mrs. Burr. When speaking of his neighbor, Isadore would smile, shake his head slightly, and with the wisdom gained from having survived trench warfare, the death of a son, economic depression, and a lifetime at the end of a dirt road, he'd say, "She plants radishes and expects to grow daisies." For a farmer from an era when the term "organic farming" was redundant, this was the ultimate metaphor for foolishness. You see, Frau Burr was never happy, but, as Herr Schraufnagel was quick to point out, she never put happiness in the world, so what did she expect?

We, of course, understand the common sense of cause and effect. None of us would ever plant radishes and expect daisies. We wouldn't scatter thistle seeds hoping to cultivate strawberries. Or would we?

Our thoughts are the seeds of our experiences, so we should be very mindful of what we think. Using a bit of exaggeration to emphasize his point, Jesus says don't wait until you commit murder to realize you're on the wrong side of the street. As soon as you're angry with your brother, you've chosen to walk on the dark path. Don't wait until you're in the throws of adultery to realize you have a problem. As soon as you venture onto the wrong websites, you're heading in that direction.

The message has three very important implications critical to happiness. First, we have to admit we're sinners. It's part of our nature. Who hasn't ever gotten angry at someone? Who doesn't get ticked off once in a while, maybe even delighting a little darkly when someone finally gets a comeuppance? It's part of who we are as humans. These thoughts will not lead to peace and happiness; they only lead to hurt. Radish seeds yield radishes, and thistle seeds yield thistles. So we need to be aware of what we're planting in our minds and cultivating in our hearts.

The second implication is that once we admit we've had these thoughts, we can never again judge someone else. We've walked on the same path. Now, we might have turned back before we went as far, but as Jesus points out, that doesn't give us the right to go around thinking we're morally superior. We've sown the same seeds.

And the third implication is that we need to practice mindfulness. Our thoughts determine who we are. We become what we think. If we walk with negative thoughts, we become negative people. If we think critical, hurtful, or defeatist thoughts, we become critical, hurtful, or defeatist people. Likewise, if we think joyful, compassionate, and encouraging thoughts, we become joyful, compassionate, and encouraging people.

It sounds so simple because it really is so simple. If you want daisies blooming in your life, the wise Herr Schraufnagel advises, then plant daisies.

Grandma's Shocking Revelation

THE CONVERSATION AT THE TABLE NEXT TO ME WAS FAR MORE INTERESTING THAN THE EMAIL I WAS READING, so I sat with my hot chocolate, looking at the screen but listening to the grandmother and her granddaughter just a few feet away. Part of me felt uncomfortable, fearing my eavesdropping was an invasion of their privacy. But they were making no attempt to speak in hushed tones, and one can't help but overhear in a crowded coffee shop.

From what I pieced together, the younger of the two was home from college and they were spending the day together in celebration of her grandmother's seventieth birthday. Their dialog had a wonderful ease, a warm comfort that boosted my faith in humanity. Topics skipped across the surface: news of relatives, classes at school, memories that seemed long ago for the granddaughter but just a whisper ago for the older woman. I perked up when the young woman asked her grandmother about her own college experiences in the late 1960s.

"Were you part of the hippie culture, Grandma? Did you wear bell-bottoms and all that?"

"I got a pair for Christmas. I thought they were so groovy, but I couldn't wear them to class. I went to an all-women's Catholic college, so we had a strict dress code."

More questions about the older woman's life were proffered. Did you date anyone before Grandpa? When you started nursing did you have to wear one of those white caps? What are your favorite memories of raising kids? And then came the kicker, "What was the hardest thing you ever had to face?"

"Oh, that's easy. It was when your grandfather died."

"I was so young. I don't really remember that. How did you get through it?"

The older woman took a sip from her coffee and set the cup down on the table. "My faith. I don't think I could have gotten through it without my faith."

"Grandma, I didn't know you're religious." The younger woman perked up in surprise. "You never go to church."

"No, I'm not very religious." She picked up her cup again and wrapped her hands around it but didn't lift it to her lips. "But my faith means everything to me. You know, my mother was a very religious woman. She drilled it into us. But there was no real depth to it; she was religious but not at all spiritual. And since she never seemed happy, I thought I'd try things the other way around."

I was struck by how smoothly her matter-of-fact tone blended with the sincerity and love obviously being shared. How do you convince a young person embarking on life's journey that the church offers something of value when her own grandmother is telling her that she has found a lifetime of faith outside of the church?

When we among the churchgoers hear claims of being spiritual but not religious, we're tempted to roll our eyes derisively. But how did religion and spirituality become separate, distinct things? It's easy to blame secularism and individualism, but that seventy-year-old grandmother's comment hit me hard: "My mother was religious but not at all spiritual, so I decided to try it the other way."

Is it possible that we, the religious churchgoing folks, are the ones who first separated religion from spirituality? Have we shown the rest of the world that it is possible to be religious without being spiritual so, by consequence, it must also be possible to be spiritual without being religious?

Jesus had a problem with the some of the Pharisees because, even while they were devoutly religious, they had a tendency to prioritize form over substance, rules over compassion. How do we measure up? If we profess our love for God without practicing love for neighbor, we might be religious but not always spiritual. If we receive Holy Communion in the church but don't become Holy Communion in the world, we might be religious but not spiritual. If we pray for peace but harbor hatred, pray for forgiveness but judge others, or pray for the poor while profiting from systems that create or exploit poverty, we might be religious but not spiritual.

It's great to gather like the disciples in the upper room, to come together, share our stories, and support one another. We need to do that. But we can't hide out in the religion and keep our faith small. Work needs to be done out in the world. "As the Father sent me, so I send you." Our job as Christians is to lead lives that so joyfully integrate our religious practice in the church with our spiritual presence in the world that no one would ever think to separate the two.

Syrup with Pancakes

On a brisk November morning, the crisp wind blew me into the Main Street Café in Viroqua, Wisconsin. From the pancakes and eggs on the menu to the faux oak paneling on the walls, everything was exactly as it would have been during the Carter, Ford, and perhaps even Nixon administrations. I imagine the coffee was poured from the same pot in the same way, perhaps even by the same person wearing the same avocado apron.

Settling into an overly comfortable booth, I noticed an aging couple across the way sitting next to one another on the same side of the table. They looked as though a photo director had called central casting and ordered a couple from the rural Midwest that's been married fifty-five years. I wondered how many times before they had sat together in that same booth. It's the sort of romantic positioning typically reserved for young teenagers in love but soon replaced by the more conventional face-off arrangement whereby a husband and wife take sides at the table as though entering a negotiation. Here, on an island of time where there is nothing but routine, the relationship shared by this couple wrapped the air like grandma's quilt.

Will I know that sort of love in another twenty-five years? In our late seventies, will Michelle and I cozy up on the same side of the booth to sip orange juice and discuss the morning news? Will we find ageless comfort in finishing one another's sentences as though speaking one thought through two mouths? I like to imagine we will. But it takes courage to express love in public, and it takes even more courage to transcend self and enter into oneness with another. Sometimes it takes more courage than I have.

The marriage that truly inspires is not one that cozies up on the same bench but one that has pilgrimed through the storms of life in an effort to arrive at such a place. Our faith benefits so much when we see a lifetime of love sitting side-by-side in an endless moment unfettered by a culture addicted to transition. Who needs a retirement condo in Florida if you know the warmth of Christ in the person sitting next to you in Viroqua's Main Street Café?

I'm sure their marriage has not always been a story of side-by-side harmony. Their matching weathered faces and gnarled hands told a story of grit, experience, and perseverance. The right to lean against each other and steal bits of sausage off each other's plate has been well earned.

In an era that defines itself by divisions—conservative vs. liberal, orthodox vs. progressive, English speaking vs. Spanish speaking, gay vs. straight, etc.—a man and a woman have committed themselves to a lifetime of love for each other. And that's a beacon of hope for all of us. There will always be arguments about money, sharing housework, intimacy, bad habits, and all the other stuff that tests love's resolve, but if we live it and let it, love conquers all. The differences fade; the love transcends. For me on that morning, seeing love shared in such an ordinary way by such ordinary people in such an ordinary place was a Eucharistic moment. What better expression of holy communion can there be beyond a lifetime of persevering love?

St. Paul was inspiring when he wrote that love is gentle, love is kind. But love is also simple. It's as simple as sitting next to one another on the same side of the booth, as simple as walking hand-in-hand through the toothbrush aisle at Target, and as simple as picking my dirty laundry off the floor so my bride doesn't have to look at it. Perhaps if I want more love in my life, I need to make room for more simplicity.

There Are No Foam Fingers in Heaven

THE WISE EDITOR WOULD ADVISE THE FOOLISH AUTHOR TO AVOID CONTROVERSIAL TOPICS, OR AT LEAST TO PROCEED WITH GREAT CAUTION. But sometimes truth demands we muster the courage to wrestle with a divisive issue, particularly one that has spurred many dinner table arguments for the past thirty years. Namely, this: How should the National College Football champion be determined? Back in 1998 there was an effort to resolve the issue through the Bowl Championship Series. That just created more arguments. Now, of course, we have a college playoff system, but only four teams qualify, so there is still a great deal of controversy. And people get animated. Oh, man!

When caught in the crossfire of these debates, I usually ask, "Why does it matter? Why do we need to know who is number one?" And when I ask this question, people look at me as though I had just pledged my allegiance to Gozar the

Gozarian. We Americans are obsessed with ranking things. Just for kicks, I typed "top ten list" into the Google machine and I got over 131 million hits. We rank everything and everyone. From preschool video games to the world's best whiskey (1989 Old Pulteney), we have a compulsive need to identify who or what is first, second, third, and so forth. Someone once approached me after Mass with his list of the top five preachers in the diocese and then offered tips on how I could make the list. It's so ingrained that we can't even imagine it being otherwise. We need to know who's Number One!

This need to be Number One is such a big part of our culture that we believe it actually matters. We think it has value, so we compare ourselves to see where we rank: How does my household income stack up? Where does my IQ rank? In what percentile is my child? And as soon as we start to compare, we start to label: Who's a winner and who's a loser? Who's a success and who's a failure? Who is a VIP and who can be ignored? First, we compare; then, we compete; and then, we condemn.

Not only do we build ourselves up, we often do so by tearing others down. In our effort to elevate and impress, we stigmatize and villainize. This is happening all across our land. Democrats bashing Republicans. Republicans bashing Democrats. Awful, terrifying things are said about immigrants, Muslims, women, people who are transgender, people who work on Wall Street...basically anyone who looks different, thinks different, or acts different from us. We willingly tear them down to raise ourselves up.

Jesus looked around and saw the same thing, but he refused to participate. Instead, he taught by parable and example.

Instead of raising yourself up and putting others down, seek to raise others up and humble yourself. Become the foot washer. Seek not to be served but to serve.

That all sounds nice, but how do we do it? We can start by replacing possessive language in our thoughts and conversations with submissive. We tend to think in terms of "my time," "my talents," "my resources," "my life." This is actually a self-centered way of seeing our place in the world, starting with me. What if everything I think I have actually belongs to God? God's time? God's talent? God's resources? God's life? What if I'm merely the caretaker?

The truth, and maybe this is the part where things really do get a little controversial and uncomfortable, is that everything we have, every moment of time, every beat of our heart, every breath we take, is indeed on loan from God. Earth is a temporary address, a cosmic homeless shelter. We possess nothing.

Good Morning, Sunshine

THERE WAS NOTHING REMARKABLE ABOUT BOB DEFRIES, AT LEAST NOT FROM THE OUTSIDE LOOKING IN. Bob lived in a humble home on a tree-lined street with Becky, his wife of many years. Every morning Bob kissed Becky and drove ten miles to the cheese factory where he worked for many years. An ordinary man, an ordinary job, an ordinary life, at least from the outside looking in.

On the Saturday of a Labor Day weekend, Bob gave Becky a kiss and went fishing. As he launched his boat, the rope slipped from his hand and the small vessel drifted away. Bob waded in after it. But there was a drop off and Bob couldn't swim very well. A couple hours later, a police officer knocked on Becky's back door. Bob had drowned.

Again, there was nothing remarkable about Bob, at least not from the outside looking in. Yet everyone, and I do mean everyone, turned out. On the night of Bob's wake and vigil, a long line twisted around the block. Family, friends, people who worked with Bob, neighbors, relatives, church members—they all came. And all wondered how this soft-spoken, unassuming man in a small town could possibly have known so many people? A thousand people who didn't know one another stood together in line for two hours to pay their respects, each knowing how the others felt, because they all knew Bob. At the funeral, the church was packed to the rafters. It was a remarkable outpouring for a man who wasn't all that remarkable, at least not from the outside looking in.

But one woman, Alice, who's own life had experienced more than its share of pain, summed up everyone's story with her own. She introduced herself to Becky and confessed she really didn't know Bob all that well. She just happened to punch the factory time clock every morning at the same time he did. Every day, month after month, year after year, no matter how dark and dreary her own life was at the moment, Bob would smile and, with a twinkle, look her straight in the eye and say, "Good morning, Sunshine." There were many days, she said, when that was the lone bright spot. Good morning, Sunshine. And if you knew Bob, you could just hear the words roll from his smiling mouth in his dry but perpetually upbeat tone.

Bob was a good man by all counts and he attended Mass every morning before going to work, but he wouldn't have cut it by the standards of the self-righteous or law-obsessed then or now. He just didn't live that way. He ate too much of the wrong stuff, didn't shy away from the deep fryer, and sometimes he laughed at the wrong jokes. But Bob absolutely was a disciple by the standards of the gospel. He never gave a second thought to what the world gave him but instead focused all his attention on what he gave to the world. And he gave it everything. Maybe there wasn't anything remarkable about Bob from the outside looking in, but from the inside looking out, wow! His simple, unassuming life touched thousands of people.

How different would our world be if we lived like Bob? We tend to be more pharisaical than we care to admit. We pay very close attention to what gets into ourselves from the outside world. We worry about calories, cholesterol, and trans fats. We buy lottery tickets in an effort to get more of what's "out there" back to ourselves. And we obsess over how others in the world treat us personally.

In the midst of it all, we forget that the most Christian life we can live is the life that notices and reaches out to other people, the life that looks people we barely know in the eye and says, "Good morning, Sunshine."

Didn't Plan
Any of This

I WONDER IF DAVID'S BIRTH WAS PLANNED. It strikes me as unlikely. I doubt his parents would have hired a babysitter for the other nine children so they could go out for dinner and have a heart-to-heart about whether to try for a tenth.

"Honey, how many kids do you want?"

"Well, we have two girls but only seven boys. Let's plan on at least one more."

"But odd numbers are better for family portraits. Maybe we should get a dog instead."

Nah, the birth of David, history's most famous king, probably wasn't planned. He wasn't intentionally raised to be a great king, either. It's fair to assume his mother didn't listen to Mozart for Mommies when she was pregnant, his parents didn't enroll him in a prestigious preschool, and he didn't attend expensive King Development summer camps. Instead, he was sent into the fields to watch the sheep. And that was good enough for God. David represented the sort of raw, earthy clay God could work with.

It's very different from how young couples approach parenthood today. What was once good enough for God's chosen king apparently is no longer good enough for *our* children. We now plan children like vacations, making sure every detail is as perfect as possible; and we regard them as achievements, as though they represent career accomplishments. A life of muddling through middle-management can be redeemed if your kid gets a baseball scholarship. It's not enough to simply raise our children lovingly; we have to raise them competitively.

I wasn't planned. Some would even say I was a mistake, or certainly what many have come to call an *oops* baby. My parents already had two children under the age of two, and as a young couple trying to live on an inexperienced carpenter's wages, they were, by all measures, quite poor. The last thing they needed was the stress and demands of another infant in the house. I was an inconvenient truth. Yet they welcomed me and they loved me. Within the last couple of generations, we as a culture have moved away from this idea of welcoming God's children, and we have replaced it with this notion of wanting our own children.

We struggle with this distinction between *having our* children and *raising God's* children. We often believe we have a right (if not even an obligation) to create our kids in our own image rather than nurturing them to reveal God's image. And it's not just what we do to our kids; we do it to ourselves as well. We devour motivational messages telling us to focus on what we want, set goals for the self, and network with people who can help us achieve those goals. It's all about self-advancement. If Mary and Joseph had bought into this ethic, they would have said no to God, not now, not then, and not there, and not among these people. Raising God's child wasn't in their plan.

When I think of people in my life who have been the truest, deepest blessings, I must admit I did not plan on any of them being there. Somehow, they found me or I found them. Whether through the mystery of the Spirit, the hard work of angels, or the funky way the universe manages to work things out, hundreds of people have inspired, comforted, challenged, encouraged, educated, nurtured, and loved me when I needed it most. I have not orchestrated any of it, but I have tried to be open to all of it. Perhaps that's the difference between a life based on planning and a life based on discerning. When we plan, we start with what we want and close off other options. When we discern, we start with an open heart and listen to the whispers of the Holy Spirit.

Think about all the people who've entered your life and what a blessing many of them have been to you. Yet, I'm guessing you planned on meeting very few of them. When we set aside our own conveniences, when we set aside what we want and welcome what God wants for us, amazing, joyful blessings come our way.

Who Cares About the Score?

WE PLAYED A LOT OF KICKBALL WHEN I WAS A KID. That was before human ingenuity figured out how to play games on TV screens. Why risk grass stains when you can "kick" a yellow pixel with a blue pixel controlled by your thumb? The world of my childhood was so primitive we had to play games on two legs in a backyard where all the neighbor kids gathered. The black walnut tree was first base, a mud patch was second, a honeysuckle bush was third, and a square in the sidewalk was home. We had no referees, and there were no parents in lawn chairs except on Sundays, but they paid no attention to us.

When you showed up, you got put on a team. Period. Age, size, gender didn't matter. Even the tag-along little brothers and sisters were placed on a team and given a chance at bat. They were never called out, but their runs didn't count.

Now, it wasn't always as utopian as nostalgia likes to pretend. Fights inevitably broke out. You're out—Am not—I got you!—You missed by a mile—What are you, blind?—What are you, stupid? Then the whole game broke into fights and name calling until someone finally said, "Let the babies have their way." But one kid in the neighborhood, Scott, who was in my grade but always seemed older, never argued. If an opponent called him out, he just accepted it even if he was obviously safe. It drove me nuts! So one day when he was on my team, I confronted him:

"Why did you let them call you out? You were safe!"

"Because," he replied, "we'd end up in a big fight. It ain't worth it."

"But two runs would have scored!" I protested.

"So? Who cares about the score?"

"Who cares about the score?! That's why we play!"

"Look," he said, "in fifteen minutes we're gonna all get called home for supper. The score won't matter. In a lousy fifteen minutes we're all going to get called home, so let's not waste it fighting with each other. Just relax and have a good time."

While the rest of us were wasting our time and energy with petty self-interest, Scott was playing the long game. Whether he was being pragmatic or was, in fact, a twelve-year-old philosopher, Scott was sharing a valuable perspective.

This idea of turning the other cheek is not about surrender or giving in: it's about playing the long game; it's about staying so focused on the reason we're here—to love one another— that we simply don't allow our heads and hearts to become possessed by the anger and pettiness that divides us.

In the grand scheme, the idea of fighting fire with fire escalates conflict. That's why the fire department uses water and doesn't bring blow torches and flame throwers to a house fire. The only way to extinguish the flames of hatred, anger, and violence is with the baptismal waters of love, mercy, and forgiveness. Because, truly, love and only love conquers all. So let's not worry about the score. Just play the long game with all our heart. In fifteen minutes, we'll all get called home for dinner.

Part Four

EXAMINATION

A Poke at the Pops

A FIGHT BROKE OUT AT THE BOSTON POPS ON AN OTHERWISE
ORDINARY FRIDAY NIGHT. It was a typically sedate, seemingly sophisticated crowd of music lovers dressed to the nines
for opening night. Women in gowns, men in tuxedos, glitz,
glamor, and all the trappings of sparkling refinement.

Apparently, one gentleman tapped the shoulder of a fellow
patron and requested the honor of his silence during the performance. It seemed reasonable, as one customarily attends
a concert to listen, not to chat up those around you as one
might during a baseball game. When this initial overture was
ignored, a second was issued. As an expression of gratitude
for the etiquette reminder, the talkative gentleman offered
to catapult the gentleman who had requested silence over
the balcony rail and onto the floor seats at Symphony Hall.
According to witnesses, his tone lacked grace, and his com-
position was without melody. An usher was notified. Upset
that his threat had been reported, the offending gentleman
performed a percussion solo on the chin of the first man. Thus
ensued a fugue-like fist medley of sorts.

Tavern-esque brawls such as this, once reserved to poker
cheats, jealous husbands, and drunken sailors, have become
increasingly common. Disagreements become conflicts, conflicts become arguments, arguments become fights, and fights
turn violent all within the fluid motion of a hat drop. From
parents punching youth baseball coaches to guns fired in road
rage, the cool head of civility has been usurped by omnipres-
ent anxiety. We live in fear that the person across from us is a
timebomb one tick away from Armageddon. What gives?

We might begin to understand by considering the nature of violence. The best definition I've come across was shared by the staff of a domestic abuse shelter. It described violence as any action or attitude that compromises the dignity of another person. In other words, when we ignore, disregard, or otherwise diminish the sacred dignity of another person, we are actually engaging in an act of violence against that person. By this definition, issuing "the bird" while driving, pornography, racism, homophobia, psychological manipulation, economic injustice, even gossip are all forms of violence. In action, expression, or attitude, they devalue another person. In the Boston Pops example, the violence didn't begin with the punch to the chops. It started by ignoring the request to be respectful of the patrons seated nearby.

Even the briefest cultural observation reveals a deep and wide problem. Violence has permeated our social psyche, emotions, and attitudes. How readily do we marginalize and stigmatize "the other" by judging, avoiding, or labeling anyone who doesn't look, think, act, vote, or worship as we do? Instead of affirming someone else's human dignity, we choose to diminish those who aren't like ourselves. We should not be surprised, then, when it escalates and is acted out.

Has our ego-driven spiral into individualism led us to a place where human dignity, even personal dignity, is readily compromised? Have we become so self-absorbed that we don't hesitate to objectify others? Christian faith, which often offers more wisdom than it gets credit for, teaches us that every human being is sacred. We are thereby challenged to view anything that denies the sacredness of another human as violent.

Of course, you and I aren't going to heal all of society. At least not in the short term. But we can start with our own hearts and our own homes. In our attitudes, our thoughts, and our dialogues, we can affirm the sacred dignity of all human beings...but only if we choose.

⊸⊱⊱⊱⊱⊱⊱⊱⊱⊱⊱⊱⊱⊱·⊰⊰⊰⊰⊰⊰⊰⊰⊰⊰⊰⊰⊶

Ratted Out by Tonka Tracks

BEFORE SAUL EVER STRADDLED HIS STEED AND TROTTED TOWARD DAMASCUS, before he bonked his bean and had his come-to-Jesus moment, even before his dark career chasing down Christians, he was just a Jewish kid who played in the dirt. He got a few small perks because his family had become Roman citizens, but it wasn't much. For example, the lunch lady at Tarsus Octavius Elementary would slip him an extra carton of chocolate milk once in a while, but that was about as good as it got. There was nothing remarkable about him, certainly no reason to think this particular skinny boy would grow up to become one of the most influential people in human history.

His mother encouraged him to become a doctor so she could brag to the other women gathered at the well. She badgered him to study herbs, practice wound closure, and read what the Greeks had been writing about science. Many years later when Saul was sewing tents in Corinth, he observed that his mother's prodding to learn Greek and practice stitching had proven beneficial after all. As a kid, however, he thought it was a droll waste of time. If anything, the relatives thought he might become a construction manager or perhaps an architect. He regularly spent all day on the edge of the desert with his toy cranes and shovels, digging in the sand, moving rocks, and constructing massive rudimentary cities with temples, coliseums, and condominium complexes.

On one particular spring day when Saul was ten years old, he decided to build a city closer to a food source. "It's not realistic to build a city in the desert," he later explained to his friend Augustus "Auggie" Rabinowitz. "Seriously, who'd want to live there? You'd have to do something ridiculous like build massive casinos to get people to go there." He relocated his toy cranes, shovels, and prized Tonka dump wagon to the rich soil beneath his mother's olive trees and spent the day in the shade.

So it was that his father, upon arriving home from work that afternoon, noticed a disturbance had occurred in the olive grove a few cubits off the back patio.

"Were you playing in the olive garden?" he asked Saul at dinner that evening.

"No."

"Don't lie to me."

"Well, I drove my dump wagon around the yard."

"Did you drive it in the grove by the patio?"

"No." Who was he kidding? A couple saplings had been broken off, holes had been dug, and there were Tonka-sized wheel tracks. He was busted and he knew it.

The discipline came fast. He had broken two of the Top Ten: he had disrespected his mother via her olive trees AND he had borne false witness. He tried to negotiate the second count, arguing that he hadn't technically borne false witness against his neighbor, but his father slammed a fist on the table and stated emphatically that a lie is a lie. For digging in the olive grove, Saul was required to apologize to his mother and fill in the holes. For lying to his father, he was grounded for two weeks—no friends, no bicycle.

Well, actually, Saul wasn't grounded. He didn't even have a bicycle; they hadn't been invented yet. In fact, this isn't even his story. There are no surviving stories from Saul's childhood, so we really don't know what sort of a kid he was. Maybe he was obsessed with purity and never played in the dirt. Who knows? But this is a real story; it's my story. I assigned it to Saul because a story about a biblical figure in an olive grove is far more compelling than a story about a Wisconsin boy digging in his mom's flower garden. But that's exactly what I did on the day I decided my 128-sq.-ft. sandbox wasn't big enough. And I got caught. And I lied. And I was grounded for the lie.

The consequences of lying were always far more severe than the consequences of the original offense. Honesty, I was taught, is not optional. A man is only as good as his word. Everyone makes mistakes, but only scoundrels lie about them. Time and again my father drilled into me the notion that honesty is the cornerstone of character. I grew to value truth as the beacon of a moral life and deceit as the marker of a sinful life.

Apparently, this was not the code with which we were all raised. We now live in a world in which bold-faced lies and brazen deceit are passed off as fake news and alternative facts.

It is a strange culture for someone like me. Fabrications and fictions are given equal and often more credence than facts. There are no consequences for lying; indeed, it is almost expected. Character seems quaint.

"Truth," Pontius Pilate scoffs, "what is truth?" In being so dismissive, Pilate illustrates that those who believe truth is arbitrary are capable of any sort of evil, up to and including killing Christ himself. We live in tenuous and even dangerous times not far removed from Jerusalem in AD 34. The greatest threat we face may not come from potential terrorists, rogue governments, or guns on our streets. Truly destructive forces destroy from within, starting with a willful disregard of the truth.

Mercy from Three-Point Range

WHEN YOU SHOOT HOOPS IN WHITNEY PARK, YOU PLAY BY NEIGHBORHOOD RULES. That's just how it is. For the most part, those rules are the same for everyone. Except Tamious. As a scrappy seventh grader, Tamious is noticeably smaller in stature but bigger in spirit than everyone else on the court, including his middle school peers. His hand-me-down sneakers seem awkwardly clownish on his slender frame, but he plays with a broader smile and has more fun than the tallest, the fastest, or the strongest.

Here's what you'll need to know if you ever "ball" at Whitney: Tamious gets to travel and you're not allowed to block his shots. Period. That's not negotiable. Now, no one is going to tell you this. You're supposed to figure it out on your own. At first it seems a little odd. He'll take a pass, tuck the ball under his arm, and scamper like a tailback. When he squares to shoot, everyone backs off and lets him gun it. Maybe he'll make it. Probably he won't. No one really cares.

You don't have to play with these kids very long before you understand what's going on. Mercy. This is not your garden-variety, self-congratulatory mercy, the type where we withhold the retribution or just deserts we think someone deserves. No, this is pure mercy born of love and offered with joy.

We typically think of mercy as a generous gift offered post-judgment when someone has done something hurtful, harmful, sinful, or dangerous. At these times we feel quite justified in judging the action as wrong, but when exacting consequences we "have mercy" and reduce or perhaps even eliminate the penalty. This may seem like a compassionate expression of human mercy, but it is still an exercise of one person exerting power over another. Whether we levy or suspend punishment, we remain the arbiters of power and control. True mercy is rooted on a plane far above the whole power equation. It is about respect and dignity. It lovingly honors the inherent sacred value of each person.

Most of the kids in the Whitney Park pick-up games have seen a lifetime of pain and struggle before they're old enough to shave. They understand and, more important, they respect, the unique life challenges each person faces along the journey. While the rest of us may be merciful when exacting judgment, these kids are merciful instead of issuing judgment. They offer mercy to Tamious not because he needs it or deserves it but rather because they want it. He is one of them, part of them. The joy of the game and the time shared together have more value than the rules or the competition. In addition to being kind and generous, mercy lightens a darkened world.

The exception granted to Tamious reflects how these kids believe the world ought to work. Their mercy is not the fair thing to do or the just thing to do; it is the loving thing to do. Viewed through their eyes, life is hard. The journey is difficult. People need a break. From this perspective, mercy toward one is hope for all.

There Ain't No Lead Up There

UNLIKE MOST OF THE BOYS IN THE NEIGHBORHOOD WHERE I GREW UP, I DIDN'T GET PAID FOR MOWING THE LAWN. This struck me and my twelve-year-old colleagues as a grave injustice. When I appealed the issue at dinner one evening, I was told that it's unfortunate the neighbors regarded their children as hired labor. Unlike them, my father explained,

"You're not hired to mow the lawn; you're expected to mow the lawn." I objected, of course, accusing my father of leveraging a technical distinction to exploit free labor. Actually, I'm giving myself more credit than I deserve. What I really said was, "That's not fair!"

He set down his fork and leaned in. This was a man who prominently displayed a small poster in the back window of his truck with an illustrated proctologist telling his beleaguered patient, "I don't care what your boss says, there ain't no lead up there." For my father, work was a matter of pride and dignity. He finished chewing and took a drink of milk. I held my breath while he drew his. "You are part of this family," he said. "As part of the family, you're expected to help out and contribute. We don't pay people to be part of the family." I needed to mow the lawn, I was told, because that's how I could contribute to, and not just take from, the family.

It was a rather radical perspective on work, which I would eventually pass on to my own children. Work is not something we do just for a personal reward or a paycheck; it's something we do to contribute in a way that ultimately gives us a sense of value and dignity. This, perhaps, is the foundation of vocation. As such, it is a value and a privilege.

Looking around, I sense my father's perspective has become quaint in the way a butter churn is considered both admirable and old fashioned. We seem to have devolved into a population that thinks personal gain is the only reason to work. So when we're asked to go work in the vineyards, we say, "what's in it for me?" And then we either just say no like the first son in the parable of the two sons (Matthew 21:28–32) or we just don't bother to show up, like the second son.

During the Great Recession, I read a fascinating article by an economist and professor of financial ethics who surmised that the financial crisis in America resulted from an economy that focused on the creation of wealth for individuals rather than the common good and sustainable growth. In other words, we got in trouble because we base success on how much of the pie we get for ourselves rather than on how big of a pie we help create for everyone to share.

Now I don't know enough about macroeconomics to agree or disagree, but I do know that I was taught two important things: First, it's better to give than to receive, and it's better to serve than to be served; and second, as my father used to tell me, never do anything just for the money, or you won't find happiness.

We're all called to go work in the vineyard. We all hear the whisper of the Holy Spirit from time to time. "Go visit that elderly neighbor who lost her husband a couple years ago." "Bake some cookies and take them to that single mom across the street. Gosh, she must feel overwhelmed." "Volunteer to help coordinate the upcoming Habitat for Humanity build." "Step out of your comfort zone and go read to residents at a nursing home." It's a different call for each of us, but we all know deep inside that we hear it and that it's meant for us.

The question is whether we ultimately respond like the first son or the second son in the parable. The second son heard the call, said, "Yes...I'll do that...sometime...maybe later...after the kids are grown...when I have the time." But he never does. There's nothing in it for him, so he doesn't show up. Or will we respond like the first son, who says, "Oh, gosh, I don't think so. It's not in my plans," but then steps back and thinks about it, maybe prays about it, and realizes the call to work in the vineyard has nothing to do with what he wants or with what he'll get from it. Rather, it's about giving of his time and energy to contribute to his family and community. So he goes.

He goes because his heart is opened and his mind is changed. He gets the lead out and he gets to work. He responds to the call, not because he has something to gain, but because he has something to give. And really, don't we all?

⟿⟿⟿⟿⟿⟿⟿ · ⟾⟾⟾⟾⟾⟾⟾

We All Need More Leon

LEON SAYS WE SHOULDN'T FIGHT. It's just not cool. Actually, he said, "Man, all these dudes gots to just let the brothers be. No good comes from bustin' up a dude just cuz he be laying down smack on your rep or cuz one of his boys rolled one of yours. You gots to be chillin, an' let it go. Know what I'm sayin?" Yeah, I know what he's saying. We have to forgive one another. But sometimes it's so hard.

I met Leon one night in Whitney Park. He had been out for a walk and was on his way home. If life had dealt me the same cards that it dealt Leon, I might be more than just a bit jaded and bitter. Truthfully, I'd likely be dead. "Where I'm from," Leon told me, "most homies don't go twenty-one less they be in the pen." He's not wrong. In many urban areas, young men come of age believing they'll be murdered or incarcerated before they're old enough to order a beer at a ball game.

Yet Leon smiles widely and plays his cards as best as he can. He moved his family (two daughters and a niece) to Green Bay because he wanted to, in his words, "give my three ladies a chance." He works hard in a meat packing plant, and he worries a lot about his girls. Mostly, Leon is concerned about the messages they get from the broader culture, messages telling them they have to have wealth to have worth and that anger and hatred give people respect and power.

As I look around, I think the world could use more Leons. I wish he would put on a conflict resolution seminar, and I wish every person would be required to attend, with one exception: the Amish grandfather in Pennsylvania. He doesn't need it. In fact, he could be Leon's co-presenter.

On October 2, 2006, Charlie Roberts, a local milk truck driver, walked into the West Nickel Mines Amish School near Lancaster City, Pennsylvania, where he shot ten girls between the ages of six and thirteen. "I'm angry with God and I need to punish some Christian girls to get even with him," he proclaimed prior to opening fire. Then he committed suicide. The close-knit community of three thousand was shocked, devastated, and heavy with grief.

From this carved-out corner where there is no relationship between wealth and human value, the Amish grandfather of one of the victims gave America a huge dose of Jesus. Just hours after the shooting, this sage offered wisdom to his community and a teaching moment to all of us. "Don't let yourselves be filled with hatred," he instructed the young people mourning the murder of their sisters and friends. "We must forgive the one who trespasses against us." That's the Amish way, and dare I say the Christian way, of saying, "No good comes from bustin' up a dude." That same afternoon, Amish neighbors visited Charlie Roberts's family to comfort them in their grief and pain. And at Charlie's funeral, Amish mourners outnumbered the non-Amish.

Leon gets it. No good comes from bustin' up a dude. The Amish grandfather gets it. Don't let yourselves be filled with hatred. But do we get it? When we're hurt, do we have the depth of spiritual health to forgive those who trespass against us? Forgiveness may be the most difficult and challenging thing Christ asks us to do. Sometimes it feels just too hard, but even if it takes a lifetime, it is often the only way to heal ourselves and heal our world. The prophet from the projects gives it to us straight up. We gots to be chillin' and let it go.

⟜֎֎֎֎֎֎֎֎֎֎֎ · ֍֍֍֍֍֍֍֍֍֍֍⟞

Desert Therapy

I FINALLY FIGURED OUT WHY I WAS SO AMBIVALENT TOWARD LENT MOST OF MY LIFE. It's a marketing issue. Lent is poorly branded. Catholicism has always led with the features instead of the benefits. Think about it. Lent kicks off with Ash Wednesday, which traditionally features the following: Don't eat meat, fast by eating only one full meal, give something up that you like, and get black ashes smeared on your face. That's like inviting seventh graders to a middle school dance by saying, "Feel awkward and go home crying. It'll help you develop social skills."

We would do better by focusing on the benefits of Lent. Here's my proposal: We should retitle Lent as *Desert Therapy: Forty days to a better you.* If we bundle it with a trendy weight loss/diet book (the *Judean Desert Diet*—fish and figs, no sugar), it will instantly become one of Amazon's best sellers. Actually, this is less satirical than it seems. The whole point of Lent really is *Desert Therapy: Forty days to a better you.* Lent is a time-tested ancient self-help program.

We all find ourselves stranded in spiritual and emotional deserts from time to time. Deserts of self-doubt. Deserts of despair. Deserts of loneliness. Deserts of grief. This is a very natural and unavoidable part of the human journey. When we question our self-identity, when we get lost and try to figure out what it all means, we wander through spiritual deserts as surely as the Hebrews did when they left Egypt in search of the Promised Land. This is also what Luke Skywalker did on Dagobah when he was becoming a Jedi, and it's what Jesus was doing for forty days prior to his public life. He was wrestling with who he was and what it means, and he was confronting the temptations that could knock him off his center. Over the years we learn to embrace these parched periods in our lives, to realize they ultimately bring growth.

But there's a danger lurking in the desert. When we go there, we're usually lost, confused, and feeling blue. We're vulnerable. That's when evil takes to the air and circles like a vulture. If the word "evil" seems heavy or archaic, you can call it something else. New age theory likes to call it negative energy. Star Wars calls it the Dark Side of the Force. Scripture is bold enough to call it by name: Satan. Whatever you call it, it always seems to know just how to poke at our weak spots and tempt us accordingly.

Being human, Jesus was first tempted with selfishness, as we all are. Use what God has given you, the voice tells him, for your own gain. Don't worry about sharing it with the world. When that didn't work, he was tempted with narcissism. "C'mon, Jesus," the voice says. "You're special. You're important. Command the attention of the universe onto yourself." Finally, he was tempted with power. This time the voice says, "Hey, how about if you be the one in control? Look around your little world here. God's not in control. You are." And this is where Jesus calls it by name, Satan, and puts it out of his sight. This sounds like a fantastical story, but it actually nails it. We are all tempted by something that holds us back from becoming and sharing our best selves.

It can feel scary, but we each wrestle with something. As long as we ignore it, it is free to circle back again and again, pecking away at our vulnerability. If we're going to grow, we need to deal with it like Luke Skywalker when he finally faced Darth Vader. We need to identify it and call it by name.

For a long time, I wandered aimlessly in a desert of self-doubt—a desert of perceived inferiority. There I was tempted by a mirage of false superiority, telling me I could escape this desert by judging others as inferior to me in some way. Somewhere during my mid-thirties, I finally came to see how destructive this was, so I embarked on *Desert Therapy: Forty days to a better you*. I vowed to confront and defeat this evil named Judgmentalism. Armed only with a light saber of faith, I prayed the Lord's Prayer, but at the end, I called the evil by name. Every morning and every night through forty days of Lent, I finished the prayer with "lead me not into temptation, but deliver me from Judgmentalism." By the time Easter arrived, I simply didn't have judgmental thoughts anymore. And now, many years later, I rarely feel this temptation.

So here's the invitation: name your demon. What is it that tempts you? What holds you back from letting Christ's light shine brightly through you? Selfishness? Narcissism? Power? Or something else: Judgmentalism? The twin demons Fear and Insecurity? Greed? Name the evil lurking in your desert. Every day for six weeks, pray the Lord's Prayer and finish by asking to be delivered from the specific darkness that holds you back. That will be *Desert Therapy: Forty days to a better you.*

⧫⧫⧫⧫⧫⧫⧫⧫⧫⧫⧫⧫ · ⧫⧫⧫⧫⧫⧫⧫⧫⧫⧫⧫⧫

I Don't Want to Be Your Dreamboat

OWEN SAYS GOLF IS HIS PASSION. His wife, Julia, says it's much more like a sickness. For Owen, the world disappears in the quiet of a golf course set among trees and water. He is mesmerized by the musical note of a perfectly struck drive and the hypnotic flight of a white ball against a blue sky. Julia does not understand any of this. Her bohemian nature would much prefer to spend Saturday afternoons poking through used book stores. To her, the piles of golf magazines, the streams of golf videos, and the very presence of a golf channel feel oddly cult-like. But she knows it's important to Owen, so even though it's not her jam, as she puts it, she smiles and rolls her eyes when the topic comes up. "I'm not judging," she says to Owen, even though it feels to him like judging.

For the first few years of their marriage, Owen envied couples who golfed together. He watched as they laughed on the course and sat together in the clubhouse afterward. He wanted that too. Every time he broached the subject, however, Julia demurred. "If you really want to spend time together, then come with me to the Farmer's Market," she would say with a gleaming eye. "I'd love that." So he did, occasionally. And she reciprocated by accompanying him to the driving range where she would sit on a bench under a large maple tree and read a book while he worked his way through a bucket of balls a few yards away. Then they would go for ice cream.

What Owen really wanted, however, was for Julia to fall in love with the game. He insisted that if she would just try it, just swing a club a few times, she would love it too. "Golf is something we could do to stay active together well into retirement," he offered as though his real interest was the long-term welfare of the marriage.

Out of the blue one day, she announced she had borrowed golf clubs from a coworker. "You're right in asking me to try it," she said. "I can at least do that." So they went to the driving range, where Owen coached Julia on gripping the club, addressing the ball, swinging through, and so forth. It didn't go well. There were mostly whiffs and worm burners, with only a couple of shots getting airborne.

Thinking he was giving encouragement, Owen offered, "It takes practice. You'll get the hang of it, Dreamboat."

"No," replied Julia. "I won't. It's not my thing, and I don't want to be your dreamboat." Owen stood crushed. Julia sighed and explained, "I don't want to try to become the woman you want me to be. I just want to be me. Julia. I want you to be in love with who I actually am, not with the idea of who you want me to be. Look, you love golf. I don't understand it, but I would never ask you to give it up. I don't like golf. I have no interest in it. But you keep asking me to take it up. I feel like you keep asking me to be someone I'm not."

How often do we fall in love with ideas and images of who we want others to be rather than who God created them to be? Usually we align these notions with our own preferences and comfort zones. Even when we don't say it out loud, we're thinking it: She shouldn't wear that at her age. He shouldn't have those facial piercings. They should learn to speak English. Not only do we do it to strangers, coworkers, and neighbors, we often do it to our spouses and our children. We create images in our own minds, perhaps graven images, of who we think people ought to be, what they ought to feel, and how they ought to think, and then we measure them against those images. Usually, our images are self-serving. Instead of seeing each person as created in God's image, we see them according to an image we've created.

Sadly, we even do it to ourselves, creating an image of perfection, strength, intelligence, or success and then trying to convince ourselves and others that we fit it, or else we beat ourselves up when we fall short. And, of course, we always fall short.

The people Jesus encountered when he came into Jerusalem had an image of what they thought a Messiah ought to be. The Zealots thought he should be a king like David and overthrow the Romans, thus restoring the Jewish nation to prominence. The temple priests, the Sanhedrin, and the Pharisees had an image of the Messiah as an extremely pious, reverent, law-abiding man much like themselves. They assumed he would be just like one of them. Of course, Jesus wasn't like any of them. When they realized he did not fit the image they had in their minds, they rejected him flat out. They were not able to see the Christ created directly in God's image because he did not fit their image.

Julia's words hit Owen in the chest like a defibrillator. His heart popped back to life and he was instantly reminded of why he fell in love with her in the first place. It was because she is so authentic and comfortable in her own skin, because she doesn't care about Louis Vuitton handbags or Gucci shoes, because she shares an independent spirit and riveting conversation, because she is quietly passionate and would rather save the world than conform to it. He looked at her standing before him with eyes fixed in anticipation of his reply. But he had no reply. A long moment passed. Finally, he simply spoke what he was feeling, "I love you more in this moment than I think I ever have. Let's go home."

Part Five

JUBILATION

֍֎֍֎֍֎֍֎֍֎֍֎ ֍֎֍֎֍֎֍֎֍֎֍֎

Staying Out of
Pilate's Kitchen

So much has been written about what Jesus did after he rose, about how he appeared to Mary Magdalene; how he visited the apostles in the upper room not once, but twice; how he walked with the disciples on the road to Emmaus; and so forth. We have built the world's most prolific religion around these stories. But no one has written about what Jesus did not do, the things he chose to avoid. And that might be worth exploring because we learn as much from the things he chose not to do as we learn from what he did.

First, he did not go visit Pontius Pilate. It would have made for a great scene at the end of the movie: Pilate, alone in his kitchen, reaches into the refrigerator for an apple (a literary metaphor); when he stands up and turns around, he sees Jesus sitting at his kitchen table with a broken loaf of bread and a glass of wine; Jesus looks at Pilate and with theatric irony he says, "You might want to wash your hands before you eat that." Then Pilate's face melts like at the end of *Raiders of the Lost Ark*. Everyone would leave the theater satisfied.

But Jesus did not do this. How many of us would have? When someone causes us pain or anguish, how often do we go back and revisit it in our minds, hoping they get their comeuppance? Jesus had no need for vindication or revenge. He had risen above it. Because that's what a heart of pure love does.

Second, Jesus did not pop in at the Sanhedrin. How tempted would we have been to look Caiaphas in the eye and say, "Well, well, well, it seems someone owes me an apology.

Here I am, three days later, just like I said. Now, can we talk about the money changers, the temple tax, and how you boys exploit the poor for your own benefit?"

But Jesus had no need for vindication or justification. He had risen above it. Because that's what a heart of pure love does.

Third, Jesus did not end all pain or solve everyone's problems. He did not cure every leper, end reality TV shows, or overthrow the Roman oppressors. If given the opportunity, how many of us would seize the power, take control, and shape the world the way we want it?

But Jesus did not do this. Instead, he turned us free to live our own lives, make our own choices, and deal with the difficulties and consequences of our own journeys. He had no need for power, control, or the exercise of authority. He had risen above it. Because that's what a heart of pure love does.

Finally, one thing Jesus did do that we often take for granted is that he wished people peace. When he visited the apostles in the upper room, he greeted them by saying, "Peace be with you." These were the same guys who abandoned and denied him in his hour of need, by the way. Yet he opens with, "Peace be with you." And then he repeats it a second time. In Luke's gospel, when he pops in and revisits the disciples he met on the road, he opens in the same way, "Peace be with you." This is what a heart risen to pure love does; it wishes all people the joy of living in true peace.

Better than one hundred years lived for vengeance and antagonism is one day lived for true peace. Peace be with you.

Lean Back
and Smile a Little

I PLAYED CRIBBAGE ONE NIGHT AGAINST A LARGE GUY NAMED LARRY. According to his friends Tina and Al, Larry was a championship-caliber cribbage player. He always won. I sat down across from him and watched as he shuffled the cards without looking at me. When he finally raised his eyes, he sized me up with an uncomfortable stare that felt considerably longer than it was, but certainly longer than necessary. Then, with a single slow stroke, he ran his hand over his graying unkempt beard, smiled warmly, and offered me the cut. Within the rules of Cribbage, if you cut the deck before the deal, your opponent is granted a point. I simply waved my hand in refusal, letting him know I wasn't that much of a pushover.

Larry proceeded to beat me decisively. After he pegged his winning point, Tina and Al beamed proudly as though they had parented this Cribbage prodigy. For his part, Larry leaned back, smiled broadly, and seemed to laugh a little. I felt slightly patronized.

So we played a second game. This time the cards fell my way and I won big. In fact, I skunked him. Tina, Al, and the others who had been watching were shocked. No one knew what to say. They waited for a cue from Larry, who just leaned back, smiled broadly, and seemed to laugh a little. Clearly, the outcome meant more to the minions than to him. He was equally happy whether he won or lost. It didn't matter.

It's worth mentioning that we were playing at the St. John's Homeless Shelter, where Larry was living at the time. He had lost everything—his job, his home, all his money, and even a Cribbage game. He slept on a mat on the floor of a converted gymnasium, and yet he leaned back, smiled broadly, and seemed to laugh a little.

If we Christians really believe what we profess, you'd think we'd all be more like Larry. If we really are people of the resurrection and not people of the tomb, if we believe that those who see light can walk in the dark, and if we really believe that God is love and love conquers all, then, yes, we will be happy and joyful even when the chips are down.

The prophet Isaiah tells us that no matter how bleak things might appear, all will turn out great. But do we believe it? In the letter Paul writes from prison to the Philippians, he says, "Look, I've been rich and I've been poor. I've been free and I've been in prison. My faith makes it so I can be happy no matter what." But do we believe it? And in the gospel, Jesus tells us that true happiness and joy belong to anyone and everyone, as long as we take God up on the offer. But do we believe it?

The Christian faith is optimistic. Our world, our politics, and our economics are pessimistic, but our faith is optimistic. It's a faith of hope and of dreams. A faith of promise and potential, of laughter and joy. We believe that goodness has already defeated evil, that all pain is only temporary, and that love triumphs over hate. Now, that doesn't mean we won't feel hurt from time to time. We will. In life, pain is mandatory, but suffering is often optional. Pain is a required consequence of life and loss, but suffering is a consequence of putting our faith in the wrong place and then being let down by it. We have no choice in pain, but we often have a choice in suffering.

If we believe, if we truly believe, we will look around and feel overwhelmed by what a gift life is. We will be overcome with gratitude for the sun and the rain, for the day and the night, for the smiles and the tears. We will see that every moment of life is a profound gift, and we will lean back, smile broadly, and laugh a little. We can't help but be filled with happiness and joy, whether we like it or not.

Rub Some Mud into Your White Carpets

Captain Tim Schweiger is an officer in a suburban fire department near Orlando, Florida. On a very pleasant afternoon in late spring, he and his crew were called to a fire at a house that was quite large even by local standards, where homes of 15,000 square feet are typical. As they sped toward the location with lights flashing and sirens blaring, smoke could be seen rising above the rooftops from several blocks away. Approaching the property, they could see flames lapping through the windows in one corner. This would be no cat rescue. Their training kicked in and their minds began racing. Was anyone still inside the house? What direction was the wind blowing? Had the structural integrity been compromised?

A fire had started in the kitchen and was quickly becoming aggressive. With speed and efficiency, the crew jumped from the truck and began laying hose as Captain Schweiger raced to assess the situation. But before the firefighters could enter the dwelling, a woman came running out, waving her arms frantically and screaming, "Take off your boots! Take off your boots! I have white carpets!"

Sometimes we as humans get worked up about all the wrong stuff. The woman in Florida might be an extreme case, but we're all apt to do it from time to time. We get tunnel vision and lose sight of the big picture. We lose our sense of what the Hebrews called *shalom*, what the Buddhists call *shanti*, and what we as Christians call inner peace. It all has to do with our sense of harmony with God.

The Scriptures are filled with stories of people who fell out of *shalom*. In one of the most famous and timeless stories, the greatest king in Jewish history—David—gets caught up in the tunnel vision of his own lust, falling out of harmony with God and having a soldier killed so he could take his wife. In his Letter to the Galatians, Paul warns us not to get caught up in the tunnel vision of self-righteousness. He reminds us that spiritual harmony is not achieved by focusing on the 613 rules of the Torah but rather by opening ourselves up to the big-picture teaching of Jesus Christ. Likewise, the gospels give us several stories of Jesus confronting the tunnel vision of Pharisees who have a habit of judging others for petty infractions. Our world isn't so different. I don't have to worry about loving my neighbor if I worry instead about how she dresses.

In one particular case, Jesus is forced to deal with a Pharisee who cries scandalous foul simply because Jesus allowed himself to be touched by a sinful woman who anointed his feet. Well, this isn't exactly Jesus' first rodeo, so he recognizes the bull as soon as it bellows. Harmony with God, he tells the Pharisee and us, isn't about who touches you. It's about whom you touch. This woman had touched his heart in a kind and welcoming way. And then Jesus gives us one of the most powerful, hopeful, and encouraging lines in all of Scripture. He says, "I tell you, her many sins are forgiven because she has shown great love." That's what it's all about. Her white carpets might be soiled with mud, but she welcomed others into the home of her heart.

Ultimately, isn't that great news? Because, here's the thing: we're all imperfect. We're all sinners. I've tried living a sin-free life, but it turns out I'm a miserable failure at it. We all get caught up in our own version of the white carpet—focusing only on small and insignificant things while the world burns around us. We worry about the weeds in our lawn while people are sleeping on the streets. We shake our heads with indignation at someone's bumper sticker while we are recklessly burning fossil fuels. We get worked up over adding a few pounds while six million children die of hunger every year.

But the Scriptures tell us God forgives all. Our *shalom*, *shanti*, inner peace, our harmony with God, our nirvana, our heaven is all restored when we show great love. I tell you, your many sins are forgiven when you show great love.

Blessed Are the Fumbling, Bumbling, and Stumbling

THE SUMMER OF 1981 WAS ABOUT AS SWEET AS LIFE CAN BE. Theaters were showing *Raiders of the Lost Ark*, and my car radio was blasting feel-good hits like Eddie Rabbit's "I Love a Rainy Night." Gas was $1.25 a gallon, Simon and Garfunkel reunited for a concert in Central Park...how could life ever be better? It was the summer before my senior year, and life was a six-lane freeway with light traffic and the wind at my back. I was seventeen and confident I had the answers to all life's questions, but I had no confidence in myself.

It's not so bad being an awkward boy with a weak chin and skinny arms when you're *buzzing the gut* (our term for cruising Main Street), but when you meet a girl, yikes, you just hope she sees your inside first. You hope you can charm her with your wry wit and caring heart before she notices the gap between your front teeth. Such was the case when I met Lisa at a student council camp hosted at one of the University of Wisconsin campuses. For me, it was an instant crush. Lisa wasn't just a sweetheart; she was smart and pretty, with a pleasant small-town authenticity. But I could barely speak to her without tripping over my own tongue. I felt so inadequate. Even my USC football jersey couldn't make up for the fact that all the other guys at camp were smarter, better looking, more athletic, more talented, and overall just way cooler than I was.

On Wednesday evening, a small contingency from our camp group arranged to meet for breakfast the following morning. Lisa invited me. Lisa invited me! Well, I don't know if she actually invited me so much as casually confirmed that I would be joining the group, but the electricity sparking through my nerves sure felt like it was a personal invitation. As we walked through the cafeteria line on Thursday morning, I was intent on looking cool and nonchalant. If you can't make it, fake it, right? Act like you've been here before. Yeah, a college cafeteria...no big deal. I eat here all the time.

Without even looking, I grabbed a glass from the rack and shoved it under the orange juice machine while talking to Lisa over my shoulder. It was a bold gesture...see how cool I am? I don't even have to pay attention. Immediately, sticky orange juice began splashing over my hand, down my arm, and all over the floor. I was holding the glass upside down. In an instant, the image of suave Steve crumbled under the reality of fumbling, bumbling, stumbling Steve.

What I discovered in the ensuing breakfast conversation was that authentic, broken, real Steve was actually more likable than fake Steve. Everyone laughed as Lisa shared the story about my run-in with the juice machine, but they were kind and empathetic. My escapade offered an opening for others to share their own personal stories of mindless snafus and public humiliations. We were united in admitting our bumbles and fumbles.

This is a common motif Jesus uses in the gospels: the false image of perfection verses the reality of human failures. This is good news for us. He uses it in the story of the good Samaritan, contrasting the very pious priest and the outcast Samaritan; in the story of the prodigal son, contrasting the younger son who returns in broken humility with the perfect son who stews in resentful pride; and in the parable contrasting the righteous Pharisee with the sinful tax collector.

When we hear these stories, we often ask ourselves which of the characters we more closely resemble. It can be a tough question leading toward a hard truth. But in actuality, don't we all have both personas within ourselves? Is this not an inner spiritual conflict with which we all wrestle? On the one hand, part of us wants to put on a good front and raise ourselves up. We like feeling a little high and mighty at times, even self-righteous. And sometimes we're tempted to be rather proud of ourselves, even going so far as to validate that self-pride by pointing out the flaws in others.

On the other hand, deep inside we all know the basic truth about ourselves. We fumble, stumble, and bumble, just like everyone else. We say things we shouldn't say, think things we shouldn't think, and do things we shouldn't do. We're not perfect. Far from it. And Jesus says, "You know what, it's OK. It's more than OK. No one's asking you to be perfect. Just be honest about yourself. Be genuine. Be real. Stop hiding the flaws and trying to pretend you're someone you're not."

This is a real challenge that can work either for or against the gospel. How many pious, pompous, finger-pointing Christians have we seen fall very publicly? We look at them—from televangelists caught with prostitutes to some Catholic priests and bishops—and we say, "Ha. It was all a big act. You're no better than anyone else." Hypocritical piety reduces faith to a mask.

At the same time, however, how many humble servants can we point to—volunteers in soup kitchens, teachers who pour themselves out, Salvation Army bell-ringers—who never step foot in a church? Still, we say, "Wow, there is someone giving their life to others." These people do great service to the gospel not because they preach it but because they practice it. They bring love where love is needed.

So we have both personas within us. The self-righteous Pharisee and the humble tax collector, the artificial image and the authentic reality. Which do we share more often with the world?

The Happy Sunshine Polka Power Hour

ON A SUNDAY EVENING IN LATE AUGUST, I FOUND MYSELF DRIVING THE RURAL HIGHWAYS TO LA CROSSE, WISCONSIN, A STUNNING REGION OF ROLLING HILLS AND REMARKABLE VISTAS. As I wound through timeless towns with names like Soldiers Grove and Liberty Pole, I popped through the local radio channels. As luck would have it, I happened upon the Happy Sunshine Polka Power Hour. I don't have to tell you where my tuner was locked for the next forty-five minutes. Say what you will about polka, but it's happy music. You won't hear a polka band scream angry obscenities, nor are you likely to read about an accordion player getting arrested for cooking meth. It just doesn't happen because polka people are happy people.

Between songs, listeners called the station with requests and well wishes for friends and neighbors. I got caught up in the happiness and found my heart filled with joy as it opened to these people whom I had never even met. I, too, wanted to wish Ronnie and Arnette a happy fifty-third wedding anniversary. And I shared sincere delight for Gil and Janice, who were welcoming their lucky thirteenth grandchild, who would be blessed, one listener said, if she looked like her Grandma Janice and not her Grandpa Gil.

Such is the richness of life. And such is the richness of prayer. I wonder what sort of energy we bring to prayer. Do we bring the happy energy of polka, the mellow energy of smooth jazz, or the giant energy of an orchestra performing the 1812 Overture? I'm from the '80s, so I've often identified my prayer with the band Triumph and their great lyrics, *I'm young, I'm wild and I'm free, and I've got the magic of the music in me.*

There's no right or wrong here. Different times and different situations call for different energy...as long as we bring energy to our prayer. Too often, I fear we pray with all the energy of a disgruntled middle-aged IRS auditor who missed his bus. We show up and crunch the numbers with blank faces. Prayer, really good prayer, the kind that transforms lives, doesn't come from the left side of our brains, where we calculate gas mileage and mortgage interest; it comes from deep within our hearts. It has soul. Prayer is not mechanical, and faith is not rational; it's all spiritual. We don't think it; we experience it.

Have you ever experienced prayer so intense it made you cry? Or prayer so happy you broke out in laughter? Have you ever prayed with energy so joyful that it made you stand up and start singing? A little scary, isn't it? I know lots of folks who happily belt out the Beer Barrel Polka at Milwaukee Brewers games but won't sing in church. To experience prayer that's moving, we have to let ourselves be moved.

When one of the disciples asks Jesus to teach him to pray, what he is really asking is, "How can I have a meaningful personal relationship with God?" It's not about words or postures; it's about personal connection and community—show me how to be close to God. And Jesus' answer starts with language his audience would have understood to mean, "Start by being intimate and joyful." In other words, start with the energy of a small child who is delighted to see her daddy and won't leave him alone. Try bringing that energy to prayer and see what happens.

❧❧❧❧❧❧❧❧❧❧❧ ❧❧❧❧❧❧❧❧❧❧❧

Miss Eleanor and Rueben

AT THE AGE OF EIGHTY-THREE, ELEANOR MADISON IS A STATELY, SOPHISTICATED LADY OF CONSIDERABLE MEANS, WITH A TACK-SHARP MIND AND A FLAWLESS MEMORY. She's well travelled, well read, and very knowledgeable about the world. Since losing her husband and her eyesight in a car accident thirty years ago, she has lived in an apartment in the Westminster Hotel in Spokane, Washington, a classic, exclusive hotel with bellmen and valets that was originally owned by her father. Without her sight, she keeps her world small and familiar, and the hotel staff looks out for her.

At the age of thirty-two, Reuben Whitehall has eagle-sharp eyes but a mind and a memory that are lacking. When Reuben was thirteen he stole his father's whiskey and was punished with a galvanized pipe to the left side of his head. His father went to jail, and Reuben went to a mental health center. Now he supplements his meager disability payments by selling candy bars on the sidewalk in front of the Westminster, much to the chagrin of some staff members, but to the delight of others.

On a certain Tuesday morning, Reuben was distracted by a fire truck and ran smack into the path of Miss Eleanor as she stepped out for her daily walk around the block. The ensuing scene was quite the spectacle, with half the hotel staff pouring onto the sidewalk. Reuben apologized profusely as he scrambled to pick up his spilled candy bars, someone threatened to call the police, and a couple of the front desk attendants insisted Miss Eleanor should return to the lobby and sit down. Miss Eleanor felt all the drama was excessive and undignified, and she chastised the staff for fawning over her but giving no mind to the "young man I so rudely walked into. Where is he? I should like to apologize."

Once the doormen were calmed, an odd and unlikely friendship hatched. Reuben escorted Miss Eleanor on her daily walks, which soon expanded from the block and wandered throughout the neighborhood. He loved listening to her memories of college football games, African safaris, and European trains. And Miss Eleanor delighted in Reuben's innocence and curiosity. She loved the way he described the people and cars on the street, as though he was seeing each one for the first time.

Then she got an idea. Miss Eleanor would see the world again through Reuben's eyes, and he would see it for the first time with her as his guide. They took a cruise down the Rhine, visited the pyramids, and watched whales in the Pacific. Everywhere they went, it was hard to tell who was serving whom, who was the sheep and who was the shepherd.

This is what the Good Shepherd relationship invites us to share. It's not about power or control, not about the shepherd being dominant or the sheep being submissive. It's about mutuality and shared giftedness. It's about nourishing one another with dignity, growth, and discovery.

When Jesus says, "I know mine and mine know me," he is speaking with intimate reverence. When we know someone, really know someone, we know their strengths and their weaknesses. We know their faults and their gifts. We choose to overlook the imperfections; instead, we enrich ourselves with their giftedness.

We have the opportunity to bring the Good Shepherd dynamic to all our relationships. We can be Good Shepherds with our spouses, our children and grandchildren, and our parents. We can be Good Shepherds with our coworkers, employees, and supervisors. We can be Good Shepherds with friends, neighbors, brothers, and sisters. We can be like Miss

Eleanor and Reuben and overlook the brokenness, honor the giftedness, and raise each other up.

⚜️⚜️⚜️⚜️⚜️⚜️⚜️⚜️⚜️

God's in the Dirt Under Your Nails

THE UPS GUY SHOWED UP THE OTHER DAY. At my house, he has been more of a harbinger of spring than robins, who have a way of overpromising and underdelivering. Without fail, you can count on a record-breaking blizzard about a week after seeing your first robin. But when the UPS guy walks up the driveway with the shoebox-sized package sporting a plain white shipping label from J.W. Jung Seed Company, you can smell spring regardless of the weather.

Right there, in the midst of icy March rains—seeds! Glory be, seeds! The promise of colorful gardens and bright blossoms, bees and butterflies, crisp salads with fresh-cut lettuce, and sweet peas popped straight from their pods. Heaven on earth.

I'm not into gardening. Thankfully, Michelle is. For her, digging and planting seeds in the soil—watering, watching, weeding, and waiting—is profoundly spiritual. It's not my thing, but I've grown to respect, admire, and appreciate that it's hers. The summertime gardens in our yard are always bright, bold, welcoming, and life-giving. For this, I am grateful. I am extremely blessed to reap the benefits of seeds I do not sow.

There was a time when I felt guilty about this. I felt that perhaps I'm not as good of a person—not as good of a Christian—if I'm not able to derive a religious experience from pulling weeds. It is such a noble and pure thing, the sort of activity enjoyed by people with righteous souls but eschewed by self-serving, shallow hedonists. I wondered what was wrong with me. Perhaps Sr. Mary Alice was right when I burped out loud in the first grade—maybe the devil was in me. What kind of a person does not achieve spiritual euphoria from working in a garden? The kind who gambles away his paycheck at dog fights and drinks vodka from a brown bag, that's what kind. But I tried it. And I tried it again. Working in the garden just doesn't bring me closer to God.

Such is the nature of spirituality. Each person's relationship with God is unique and personal; spirituality is simply not a one-size-fits-all thing. For Michelle, gardening puts her in touch with the divine. I don't get the same rush from it. But I find God in the practice of stringing together words and sentences that express the profound miracle of life experience. That's my thing. But it's not Michelle's. So when we walk together in the woods, she will point out every wild flower by name while I theologize on her enthusiastic response to trilliums. It's no surprise people like her better.

This is how our relationship works. We each cultivate our unique spirituality and openly share it with one another. If I were to insist that Michelle adopts my spiritual expression, or she would insist that I embrace hers, or either of us would stop sharing with the other, our relationship would deteriorate. Ultimately, isn't this how all relationships work? Isn't this how we all enter into the one body of Christ? We each nurture our personal experience with God and then openly share it with one another. In doing so, we love one another as God loves us. We create opportunities for others to reap the harvest of the seeds we sow.

Part Six

CONTEMPLATION

Esther and Lawrence in Heaven

ELEVEN DAYS BEFORE HER EIGHTY-NINTH BIRTHDAY, ESTHER LAY ON HER BED STRUGGLING WITH THE LAST SHALLOW BREATHS OF LIFE. At her side, Lawrence, her husband of sixty-six years, sat holding her hand. Their life together had not been a fairytale. There were tough times, like when they were forced to sell the farm, Esther's frequent bouts with severe anxiety, and the baggage Lawrence carried as the son of an abusive, alcoholic father. They had fought about money, sex, religion, how to discipline the children, and whether or not Esther has a right to tell Lawrence that he needs to eat more roughage. But nothing tore at their hearts and ripped at their marriage like the pain felt when their only son was killed in Vietnam.

And now, as the final moments of Esther's life were fading, Lawrence leaned in, not sure if she could hear him or not, but sensing she could, and said, "Well, you've given me sixty-six years of heaven. I guess now it's your turn." Esther's lips parted slightly and she whispered, "You...you are heaven."

They were right, of course. They could *call* it what it was because they both *knew* what it was. Life had taught them how to recognize heaven. The rest of us struggle. We grope with analogies and metaphors. We scratch our heads trying to figure out parables. What is this "heaven"? We talk about pearly gates and eternal banquets, which are nice images although not all that useful, but we don't talk much about loving another person so profoundly that you can barely breathe in between the tears. We don't talk about water fights with the kids or about laughing so hard you fall off your chair during dinner. We don't talk about prideful six-year-olds singing their hearts out in school gyms on concert night or the poetic awkwardness of prom night. Are these not also images of heaven?

Our Catechism tells us heaven is the "place" of God, but with every reference, it puts the word "place" in quotation marks so that we know it's not literal. It's experiential. It's "place" as in a state of mind or a state of being. And what does the "place" of God mean when we're taught that God is love and God is everywhere? Is heaven the place of love? Is it possible that heaven can be everywhere always? Maybe, but you read the news and can't help but think *not in this lifetime.*

As small children, we were taught that heaven is a reward for good behavior, like an eternal paycheck for a job well done. That can be a hard notion to shake, because it offers the illusion of being just and rational. But the spiritual is not limited by the rational. As we grow in our spirituality, we realize that heaven isn't a reward. Infinite love is not something you earn. It's the unconditional gift from God, the unconditional gift *of* God.

The kingdom of heaven, as Esther and Lawrence discovered, is not the absence of all struggles but rather the ability to grow through them and transcend them—the peace we experience when we trust divine love in the midst of anything and everything. Heaven is a disposition, an attitude, a perspective. It is, indeed, an ability we grow into through a lifetime of practice. And maybe that's what life really is—practice for heaven. Perhaps the question we should ponder as our heads hit the pillows each night is, "So, how did practice go today?"

The Dalai Lama famously said that if you want others to experience happiness, practice compassion; and if you want to experience happiness, practice compassion. Perhaps the same idea translates to our Christian truth: If you want others to experience heaven, practice love; and if you want to experience heaven, practice love.

Low Blocks Are for Chickens

WHILE I WAS OFF AT DEACON SCHOOL EVERY SATURDAY FOR A FEW YEARS, MICHELLE AND ALL THREE OF OUR BOYS TOOK UP TAE KWON DO. At first, it was kind of cute, so I encouraged them with fatherly high-fives and bear hugs when they earned yellow and green belts. It was neat that they were sharing the time together and learning something new. The similarities between what I was studying and what they were studying were fascinating, but the homework was very different. And they were very diligent about doing their homework.

The seemingly benign phrase, "Dad, let me show you what we learned today," became a bellwether of pain, especially as the boys got bigger and the belts got darker. It typically introduced some sort of quick twisting maneuver ending with a roundhouse kick to my midsection. Except for my youngest son. He was shorter than his brothers and his kicks landed unfortunately lower. Reflexively, I learned the first tae kwon do skill of my own: a fast and firm low block. Every time one of the kids would say, "Dad, come here. I want to show you something," I'd immediately strike a defensive posture with one arm protecting my northern hemisphere and the other protecting the southern hemisphere.

This defensive stance was a natural and intuitive posture for me because, I realized upon reflection, I had been using it most of my life whenever I heard the Holy Spirit say, "Steve, come here." I'd cover myself, blocking with verbal defenses such as *I don't have time* or *It's not in the budget.* Of course, the correct Christian posture isn't closed and self-protective. It's open and vulnerable. We need look no further than the crucifix to understand just how open and vulnerable it can be.

Those are the choices we have. We can journey through life with our guards up, always taking a step back, fearful and protected. Or we can journey through life with our arms out, open and vulnerable.

When we choose a self-protecting posture, we get lulled into being satisfied with a self-protecting morality. This morality is based on the fear of doing something wrong, something that might hurt ourselves or others. As long as we're not doing anything harmful, we can feel good about living solid Christian lives. And there's something to be said for that. It is wrong to do things that hurt ourselves, our relationships, our neighbors, our environment, and our world. But that's just the beginning. That's the morality we teach to an eight-year-old when we say "don't hit your brother," just before we enroll him in a martial arts program and teach him to kick his father.

The moral code Jesus teaches is a lot more advanced and, frankly, a lot harder. When he's giving his final instructions, he doesn't say, "Hey, keep your nose clean and follow the law." No, Jesus ratchets it way up and says, "*I give you a new commandment: love one another. As I have loved you, so you also should love one another. This is how all will know that you are my disciples, if you have love for one another.*" He doesn't tell them to stick to a passive, protective code. He tells them to open themselves up to an active, vulnerable code.

Of course, he gives us the same instruction: *As I have loved you, so you also should love one another. This is how all will know that you are my disciples.* It's not because you have a Jesus Fish on your car, or because you watch EWTN, or even because you go to church every week and bow reverently at the right time during the creed. This is how...*if you have love for one another*, if you greet every person with your arms out, open and vulnerable. Ooh, that can knock the wind out of you if you take it seriously.

We're all challenged to open ourselves up. Sometimes, people are going to twist around and catch us by surprise with a below-the-belt roundhouse kick. And we'll get hurt by it. Far more often, however, they will open their own arms in return and hold us in a loving embrace. So we have a choice to make: be governed by fear, in which case we will keep our guard up to protect from vulnerability, or we can open up to the joyful bear hugs and comforting embraces of others. Those are the choices: the vulnerability of love or the false security of fear. Having survived three sons and a spouse who all earned black belts, all I can tell you is that a lifetime of love is well worth the risks.

On the other hand, I will also tell you that the first time a guy sees his one-hundred-and five-pound wife snap a board in half with an elbow smash, it will change the dynamic in your marriage.

—⁂⁂⁂⁂⁂⁂⁂⁂⁂⁂·⁂⁂⁂⁂⁂⁂⁂⁂⁂⁂—

God Bakes
Her Own Bread

WHEN I WAS IN THE THIRD GRADE, I WAS THE PROUD OWNER OF A BIC BANANA MARKER PEN. I had bought it myself from the local Woolworth's store, and it was the coolest thing I owned. I was so proud of that pen. One day when I came back to my desk after lunch, it was missing. It was a bad day.

We took a reading test that afternoon, and halfway through the test I glanced up and noticed Bratty-Patty Swanson suspiciously writing her answers with a yellow Bic Banana pen. From that point on I couldn't focus. I got my first D ever. It was a very bad day.

At afternoon recess, Mike Wagner, who was a bit of a troublemaker, threw a snowball that hit my best friend in the face just as the bell rang. As Mike ran for the door, I hurled a snowball that glanced off his arm. When I got up to the door, Mike was waiting, and he pushed me against the wall, so I punched him in the shoulder and used a word I shouldn't have. One of the teachers pounced on us and broke it up. We both had to stay after school and couldn't leave until we shook hands and said we were friends. But on the way out, Mike leaned over to me and whispered, "My brother is going to beat you up." Mike's brother was a notorious fifth grade bully. I ran all the way home.

When I finally burst through the back door, I was engulfed in the aroma of fresh bread straight from the oven. My mother baked all our bread from scratch. This wasn't the frozen dough or bread machine variety. This was the "knead it with your own hands and let it rise under a blanket in the sun" variety. And, oooh sweet mama, when it came fresh from the oven, it was from heaven. My grandfather raised bees, and we would drizzle some fresh-from-the-farm honey that would melt into the warm bread. On that particular day, oh wow, did it feed my hunger! But it wasn't a simple physical hunger. It was a hunger for the warmth, security, and love of home. To this day, when I smell fresh bread, it takes me right back to that warmth of a mother's love for her family.

This same story is repeated far more dramatically in the Old Testament. Whether in slavery in Egypt, wandering in the desert, or in exile in Babylon, the Jews knew what it was like to hunger for the warmth, security, and love of home. Manna from heaven wasn't just about physical food; it was the manifestation of God's warm love for his children. It's what got them through the tough stuff and satisfied all their hungers.

So when Jesus shows up and says, "I am the living bread from heaven," it rocks their socks. How dare he, this flesh-and-blood human being, identify as the direct manifestation of God's love and security?

And then Jesus goes on. "If you eat my flesh and drink my blood, you'll have eternal life." Well, this too raised eyebrows, as it does among many of us today. If we listen to these words with the technical minds of our left brains, it weirds us out a little. But if we listen with the poetic minds of our right brains, we understand that he's basically saying, "If you devour who I am—my substance and my essence, what I believe, what I teach, and what I do—if you take it all into yourself (the same way I devoured the warmth, love and security that my mother kneaded and folded into her bread), you, too, will live and love beyond the bounds of time and space."

That's a big, bold statement. And it changes everything. It also leaves us with two big, bold questions: What do we hunger for? And how do we seek to satisfy that hunger?

Most of our hardships fall somewhere between having your Bic Banana stolen and slavery in Egypt. We deal with things like job loss, divorce, foreclosure, cancer, addictions, eating disorders, teen pregnancies...we deal with all of this along life's journey, and through it all, what do we hunger for? Do we hunger for warmth, security, and love? I bet we do. I bet most of us do.

And how do we seek to satisfy that hunger? Well, here's Christ breaking himself open and pouring himself out for us. "Satisfy your hunger," he tells us, "by devouring the substance and essence of who I am. Eat and drink what I believe, what I teach, and what I do. Consume and become how I live, how I die, and how I rise. This is how your hunger can be satisfied. This is how you live and love beyond the bounds of time and space."

We should take him up on that.

Dark Night of Me

I WOKE AT 3:15 AM AND COULD NOT GET BACK TO SLEEP. Tossing and turning in the dark of night, I wrestled with demons named grief, anxiety, and loneliness. A series of trying weeks had morphed into a string of difficult months, and I was feeling emotionally and spiritually battered. The bittersweet emptiness of dropping my youngest son off at college was still fresh; the wrenching grief of my father's death six weeks earlier was just beginning to take up permanent residency in my heart; and a series of setbacks at work was driving a sense of personal failure and financial peril. "It's too much!" I had lamented to Michelle the previous evening. "It's just too much to process and deal with all at one time. I miss Adam! I miss my dad! The notion that God never gives us more than we can handle is a lie!"

When dealing with personal tribulations in the past, I usually found solace and perspective by recognizing that my issues were small and petty when compared to real-world problems such as opioid orphans in America and hungry children in Haiti. But this time things were different. Turning attention away from myself to larger concerns proved counterproductive. There is even more anxiety out there! So much pain. So much suffering. So much fear. So much anger. So much hate. Where could I find peace?

Turning to prayer, I found very little comfort and no consolation. "My God! My God!" I finally called into the faint moonlight. "Why have you forsaken me?" In the cold night of my own shadow, I expressed disillusionment with this God. "I've done everything you asked of me! I've worked hard to live a loving and generous life. I've set aside my own dreams to serve you. And where are you now? You offer me no shelter, no safety, and no comfort!"

Then it occurred to me: the notion that a good Christian life would protect me from overwhelming sorrow is a self-serving fallacy. It is merely another form of the prosperity gospel, the grossly false belief that God shines earthly favor on those who faithfully follow while bestowing earthly pain on those who stray. Even while meditating on the crucifix, had I secretly believed I could avoid my own crown of thorns by being a good and faithful disciple?

Finally, out of the corner of my eye, I spotted a copy of *Dark Night of the Soul* by St. John of the Cross. It had been sitting on the corner of my desk for a couple of months, waiting for me to pick it up. In the introduction, the translator, Mirabai Starr, explains the theme of the Spanish mystic's message:

> Say what's secretly going on is that the Beloved is loving you back. That your first glimpse of the Absolute was God's first great gift to you. That your years of revelation inside his many vessels was his second gift, wherein, like a mother, he was holding you, like a child, close to his breast, tenderly feeding you. And that this darkness of the soul you have come upon and cannot seem to come out of is his final and greatest gift to you.
>
> Because it is only in this vast emptiness that he can enter, as your beloved, and fill you. Where the darkness is nothing but unutterable radiance.
>
> Say he knows you are ready to receive him and to be annihilated in love.
>
> Can you say YES to that?

Aha! The human experience of emptiness is the opening to be filled with the divine experience of love. Suffering is not a consequence; it is a beginning, like a heavenly steel plow overturning the hardened soil of our lives. The dirt must be softened, loosened, even pulverized for the life-giving water to penetrate and the seeds of love to germinate.

The only question is how deep...how deep do I want the roots of Spirit to reach into the clod of earth named me?

Ron and Judy—What a Couple of Characters

THINK ABOUT YOUR STORY—THE STORY OF YOU. If a biographer was going to write your story, would it be a plot-driven story or a character-driven story? Let me give you a couple examples to illustrate the difference. *Raiders of the Lost Ark* was a plot-driven movie. It was compelling and entertaining, but at the end of the film, the characters hadn't really grown or changed much, and you as a viewer weren't changed by it either. Compare that with the experience of watching a character-driven movie like *Schindler's List*. Certainly, the movie had a plot, but the story captured how Oskar Schindler's character evolved from a calculating businessman to someone who was on a lifesaving mission. Schindler's character drove the film's plot, and we as viewers were changed by it as well. Hopefully, we left the theater more compassionate than when we had entered. The first thing you learn in a good literature or creative writing class is that character drives plot. Character is what shapes the stories of our lives. And yet we often live the other way around.

After visiting my parents one weekend, I began pondering whether my life is character-driven or plot-driven. My father's Parkinson's had been rapidly advancing, so Mom and Dad were preparing to move out of their house and into a condo. From the outside looking in, this would have appeared to be a very difficult thing. They had lived in their home for forty-seven years. My father had renovated every square inch of that house several times over. Along with a large yard filled with trees and flowers, it was the work of his hands. This was where they raised their family; it represented the work of their lives. How could my mother just walk away from that kitchen? How could my dad leave that workshop? And yet they both seemed very much at peace. If anything, they were wondering about how they were going to unload nearly fifty years of stuff.

You see, Ron and Judy Meyer lived character-driven lives. They viewed their house, condo, or whatever, wherever they lived, as a convention of plot. And plots have a way of twisting and turning. When you live a life that is driven by the development of character rather than the development of plot, you respond to those twists and turns rather easily.

When our spirituality is in the early stages of formation, we focus so much energy on plot. We try to shape our life story by manipulating the circumstances. What will we do? Where will we work? Where will we live? Will we get married? Will we have children and how many? What will we achieve? Will we get the next promotion? Rather than developing character, we attempt to plot our lives like a dot-to-dot puzzle, moving from one thing to the next. But as we gain life experience and we face the plot twists over which we have no control—job loss, illnesses, the deaths of loved ones—our spirituality matures; we realize happiness is defined not by plot but rather by character.

This is what Paul is telling us in his Letter to the Galatians: Look, you've lived your whole life according to a prescribed plot—don't kill, don't commit adultery, make the right sacrifice in the right way on the right day, but that's not what the story of your life should be about, nor is it where happiness is found. Instead, the spiritually mature person lives a life driven by character. Love your neighbor as yourself. That's what people of strong character do. Love one another. If you're that kind of person, Paul says, the plot will take care of itself. A loving person with strong character isn't going to kill people, or rob liquor stores, or look at nude pictures of Jennifer Lawrence online.

Paul is echoing a theme we hear throughout the gospels. The plot says don't talk to the woman at the well, but the man of strong character does it anyway. The plot says don't touch the leper or heal on the Sabbath, but the man of strong character does it anyway. The plot says don't be eating with tax collectors and prostitutes, but the man of strong character does it anyway. It's a central theme for Jesus: if your life is driven by plot, you will hold tight to all the conventions, but if your life is driven by character, you will always do what is most loving. The obvious implication is that God expands in the world through character, not through convention.

Look at all the conflicts in our lives and in our world, from international terrorism to organized crime, from arguments between spouses about money to stress in the car when we leave for a family vacation. Every one of these conflicts is caused when people prioritize the manipulation of plot over the development of character. A man of strong character would not blow up buildings, and a family of strong character would not turn on each other when it rains on the camping trip.

How different would our world be if we all took the advice of Jesus and Paul and invested ourselves in developing character rather than manipulating plot? How different would religion be? How different would our lives be?

❦❦❦❦❦❦❦❦❦❦ · ❦❦❦❦❦❦❦❦❦❦❦

Potato-Draining Wisdom

WHEN I WAS SIXTEEN, I'D SKULK AROUND THE KITCHEN BEFORE SUPPER, TRYING TO GET A HEAD START ON THE ROAST BEEF BEFORE IT HIT THE TABLE. I often used this time to bait my mother into an argument of one sort or another...a little intellectual garlic to give the ensuing dinner conversation some kick. I figured the least I could do for her was make sure her life wouldn't get boring.

Just as mom was draining the potatoes one evening, I dropped this gem: "You know, I don't think I believe in God. It's kind of a ridiculous notion if you think about it." I said this partially to get her dander up and partially because it was somewhat true. I wasn't wrestling so much with the fact of God as I was with the nature of God.

"Good," she said without missing a beat. This was not what I had expected. With wisdom that could be spoken only by a woman who kneaded her own bread and sewed patches over the worn-out knees of a little boy's jeans, she continued, "Those with the deepest faith wrestle with the deepest doubts."

Those with the deepest faith wrestle with the deepest doubts. A paradox. Diabolical. I was sixteen and had just been trumped by a five-foot-two, middle-aged woman with steamed-up bifocals. There was no argument. All I could do was seek understanding. How could it be so? Doesn't faith mean the eradication of doubt? Isn't doubt a sign of weak faith?

Eventually I would learn the wisdom in this contradiction. Those with the deepest faith get there by doggedly chasing the questions and pursuing the conflict. Doubt, conflict, and debate are not contrary to faith. They are often avenues to faith. In fact, conflict is a part of faith. When we ponder an infinite God while living a finite life, we're going to feel conflicted. When we profess belief in a God who is love while living in a world governed by fear, we're going to feel conflicted. When we value selflessness but reward selfishness, when we celebrate communion but pursue elitism, when we ask God for mercy while we judge one another, when we give to the poor while exploiting cheap labor, and when we pray for peace while waging war, we're going to feel conflicted. You can't have faith without conflict. Not real faith. Not deep, meaningful faith.

Those with the deepest faith do not run *from* questions and conflicts; they run *at* them. In fact, those with the deepest faith ignite questions and conflicts.

After teaching high school religious education classes for many years, I discovered that the kids who debated and challenged everything I threw at them often ended up with a more profound spirituality than the ones who simply sat there without ever questioning. Why? Because they engaged. They sought a deeper understanding and they refused to accept superficial platitudes.

This is the gauntlet the gospel drops before us. Are we passionate enough about what we profess to believe...passionate enough to wrestle through questions and conflicts? Or do we passively walk through the motions, avoiding the difficult questions that confront us, keeping our faith in a neat, tidy box?

The choice belongs to each of us. But the cross shows us in a pretty straightforward way that serious Christianity is messy business. It's not meant to be in a neat and tidy box. You can't have true faith without conflict. And those with the deepest faith wrestle with the deepest doubts.

The Woman Who Slows the Earth

ALYSSA IS A TENDER WOMAN. Her unassuming manner and gentle voice have a disarming way of putting people at ease. Clearly, she is gifted. I met Alyssa as I was making the rounds of guests at one of our StreetLights Outreach Block Parties. I've met many wonderful people on these occasions over the years, yet I wasn't prepared for Alyssa's quiet grace.

She was sitting on a bench by the playground, humming lightly as she softly wiped ketchup from a young girl's face. It was such a motherly moment, repeated a million times a day by a million caring moms. There was a sacred oneness about Alyssa. The woman, the child, the place, and the action were not merely pieces that came together in the moment; they were bonded in singularity like the hydrogen and oxygen atoms that make the water of life.

"Did everyone get enough cookies?" I asked as I approached, noting the large chocolate-chipper in the girl's hand. "Oh, yes," Alyssa replied as the child, freed from her grasp, melted into the sea of kids on the jungle gym. I sat down, and Alyssa asked me about StreetLights Outreach, thanked us for sponsoring the block party, and mentioned that she brought her grandchildren, who happened to be staying with her. It was typical small talk, the sort you make when meeting a stranger at an event such as this. But I was drawn in and felt a need to identify what it was about Alyssa that transcended her words. Was it her calming smile? The fact that she looked much too young to be a grandmother?

(I had assumed the small girl was her daughter.) Or was it her large round eyes, set into her dark skin like portholes into a storied soul?

Nearby, a dozen or more kids scurried about the playground, yet none cried, none screamed, none bullied. There was joy and laughter; running, skipping, and jumping; but no name-calling, power-plays, or any other childhood playground politics. In Alyssa's presence, I felt what the kids felt—a calming joy, a certain harmony. I couldn't quite put my finger on it, but the world around Alyssa definitely held a different energy.

Later, as I walked past again, Alyssa was pulling together her grandchildren and getting ready to head home. She gathered two and then three, and then a couple more joined the fold. She pointed them out to me. A few were grandchildren, the others were nieces and nephews. In all, there were nine kids between the ages of four and ten, all visiting from Milwaukee, and all had been staying with her for the past two weeks. I looked at the assemblage of kids and imagined taking care of them for two weeks.

"Wow," I said. "Nine kids for two weeks. You are a stronger person than I am."

Alyssa smiled and shook her head slightly. "Oh, they're all good kids, at least when they're with me. But tonight's the last night. Everyone goes home tomorrow."

I watched as she, surrounded by her flock, made her way toward the edge of the park. How lucky those kids are, I thought. Before she left, I asked her what she will do when all the children leave and her house is quiet. Her smile beamed more broadly. "I'll take a nap," she said. "Even God needs a Sabbath."

OF RELATED INTEREST

On Becoming Bread
Reflections and Stories to Nourish Your Spirit
DR. MARY MARROCCO

On Becoming Bread is an inspiring companion for anyone seeking to discover how God is present in every moment of our lives. Steeped equally in Scripture and sound theology, each reflection reveals new dimensions of the most ordinary of day-to-day events.
128 PAGES | $14.95 | 5½" X 8½" | 9781627854443

Scripture Passages that Changed My Life
Personal Stories from the Writers of Living Faith

Ten of *Living Faith* magazine's most well-known authors each explain how meditating on the Word of God has changed their lives. Allow the lessons that they have learned to deepen your prayer experience and maybe even change your life.
112 PAGES | $12.95 | 5½" X 8½" | 9781627853569

Hanging onto Hope
Reflections and Prayers for Finding "Good" in an Imperfect World
MELANNIE SVOBODA, SND

Exploring the relationships between hope and faith, love, courage, prayer, pain, and sorrow, Sr. Melannie helps us open our hearts to hope. With short prayers and questions for personal reflection or group sharing, this beautiful, touching book is perfect for prayerful meditation.
128 PAGES | $12.95 | 5½" X 8½" | 9781627853293

TO ORDER CALL 1-800-321-0411
OR VISIT WWW.TWENTYTHIRDPUBLICATIONS.COM

TWENTY-THIRD PUBLICATIONS
A division of Bayard, Inc.